THE

WITCHES AND WIZARDS BOOK

Amaze your friends,
astound your parents,
and outwit your enemies!

L.T. Samuels

Adams Media Corporation
Holbrook, Massachusetts

For Michael, Kelly, Zach, and Sam
Believe in your magic,
with all your heart.
It's all about fun—
right from the start!

An Everything® Series Book.
Everything® is a registered trademark of Adams Media Corporation.

Published by Adams Media Corporation
260 Center Street, Holbrook, MA 02343
www.adamsmedia.com

ISBN: 1-58062-396-4

Printed in the United States of America.

J I H G F E D C B A

Library of Congress Cataloging-in-Publication Data
available from the publisher.

NOTE: All activities in this book should be performed with adult supervision. Likewise, common sense and care are essential to the conduct of any and all activities, whether described in this book or otherwise.

Cover illustrations by Joseph Sherman.
Interior illustrations by Kathie Kelleher.
Puzzles by Beth Blair.
Series editor: Cheryl Kimball

Puzzle Power Software by Centron Software Technologies, Inc. was used to create puzzle grids.

This book is available at quantity discounts for bulk purchases.
For information, call 1-800-872-5627.

Table of Contents

WORDS to KNOW

witch or wizard: one of many terms used to describe people with magical abilities

Introduction

If you are fascinated by the subject of **witches** and **wizards**, then *The Everything Kids' Witches and Wizards Book* may be for you. It is packed with all kinds of fun activities that allow you to both look and feel magical.

Have you ever wondered if you had some magical potential? In chapter 1, you can compare yourself to the witches and wizards you've read about in books or seen on television. Maybe you have a lot in common. Take our easy tests to see just how much you know about witches, wizards, and magic.

Would you like to dress up like a witch or wizard? Chapter 2 covers everything from robes to wands to broomsticks. It tells you how to make these things and decorate them to express your own individual creativity. Also, in chapter 3, you can discover how to make a Book of Magic so you'll have a special place to keep things like your magic wish list, secret spells, or photos of your magic-loving friends.

Then the fun really begins. Chapters 4 through 8 focus on lots of fun types of magic you can try. There is Whisper Magic and Word Magic, Food Magic and Friendship Magic, Animal Magic and Art Magic, Money Magic and Music Magic. There are lots and lots of different activities for all kinds of interests.

Do you think it would be great to be able to predict the future? In chapters 9 and 10, you'll look at some of the ways witches and wizards have tried to do this in the past. Do you know what your sign of the zodiac is? Have you ever read your cookie crumbs? Do you know what your magical numbers are? When you get done with these chapters, you'll be an expert!

The last chapters lay out different activities to keep you busy through a magical year. You might choose to make Ghostbuster Balls or Magical Wish S'Mores. You might start a Magic Never-Ending Tale or plant a Magic Garden. You might perform a Magic Rescue or put on a Magical Misfit Auction. Whatever you choose, you should try to have the most magical fun you can. After all, that's what this book is all about!

Chapter

Testing Your Ma

Three magical people I would like to meet:

_____

_____

_____

Three things I have in common with them:

_____

_____

_____

Seven Secret Clues:

_____

_____

_____

_____

_____

Have you ever wondered what it would be like to be a witch or a wizard? Do you love reading stories filled with magical powers and wish you had some of your own? Well, maybe you do. In this chapter, you can take some fun and easy tests to see how you measure up magically. In Three's the Charm, you'll identify the witches and wizards you like the best—and think about why they are your favorites. You'll look for Seven Secret Clues and try the Magical Search (a magical scavenger hunt). Lastly, you can take the Witch Wiz Quiz to see just how much you already know about witches and wizards.

Three's the Charm

Who are your favorite witches and wizards? Harry Potter? Mary Poppins? Sabrina, the Teenage Witch? Merlin? Even though these magic-makers are very different from each other, they still have many things in common. Make a list of the three magical people you would most like to meet. Can you think of three things you have in common with each one? For example, are you the same age? Do you both like to sing? Do you both have a black cat? Do you both like to help friends? If you're having trouble getting started, make a list of all the things you like about your very favorite witch or wizard. I'll bet you have many of the same qualities!

Seven Secret Clues

Clues to your magical potential are everywhere. Over the next seven days, look for seven secret clues to your special powers. A secret clue could be dreaming about flying, knowing what a friend is going to say before he or she says it, having something you want to happen really happen (like winning a game or getting an "A" on a test), solving a real-life mystery (like finding lost car keys), or knowing what your dog or cat wants. There are lots of possibilities. Keep an open mind, and be sure to write them down.

Were you able to find seven secret clues in seven days? If so, you may have magical potential!

A Magical Search

Successful witches and wizards need to be resourceful. Here is a list of 13 things for you to find. You don't need to buy or even collect these things; you only need to find them. If you're not quite sure what something is, ask a friend or an adult for help. In fact, invite them to search along with you. Everyone can join in the fun of the hunt, but be sure to keep track of the things you find on your own. Use logic, common sense, and, most important, your imagination. There is no time limit for this test. Just be sure to have fun—and keep your eyes open!

Three's the Charm

Can you locate the three magic makers who are exactly the same?

WORDS to KNOW

kaleidoscope: an instrument containing bits of colored glass or plastic that create an endless variety of patterns as they change position

1. Something that fizzes (like soda)
2. A spider spinning a web
3. A **kaleidoscope**
4. Something that's soft on the inside, hard on the outside (like a bottle of shampoo)
5. The brightest star in the sky
6. The smell of freshly baked cookies
7. A purple pest (like a book character dressed in purple)
8. An upside-down teapot
9. The face of an animal where you wouldn't expect to see it (like in the clouds)
10. A rainbow-maker (like a prism or a box of crayons)
11. Blue eyes that twinkle
12. Something in the shape of the moon
13. A cat, stretching

Magical word Search

See if you can find objects from the Magical Search list hidden in this letter grid. Be sure to use your imagination, because some of the hidden items aren't exactly the same as they are in the list. In fact, two of the items are pictures, not letters! HINT: Some items are listed twice, or even three times, but in different forms. There are 17 objects for you to find.

```
A M C R E S C E N T * M R * M O * O S
T B R I H O G R S * S E Y E E U L B *
O R S E L T Z E R F A * R Q * P O U M
N M F C U V P R T S ⊥ E Ⴤ b O ⊥ N B M
I F W P D E M X E P R I S M F X Z B M
C Z J S L Z F X X B A B M P X X P L M
O B O P O A B X O X S L P X O X B E M
O A R I F D L X O X X X X X T X A P I
A U A D B L A X X O O O O A X X Z S S
P R S E K M A X O O O O C O O X F A M
F A F R A X R X O X X G X X O X B X E
B T L A B P X X O O N O O O O X X R L
Z S S N S M A X X I O X O O X X B S L
F T B D N F X X H O O O O O O X X F C
A H A W O X L C X O X X X O X A R X O
S G L E Y P T L B X O O O X P P Z A O
O I P B A E F Z P B X X X P A ◉ P S K
S R E L R L E L S U L B L S A F A F I
F B L T C S G K A L E I D O S C O P E
O P S R A L G O F A U F R A F R O A S
```

Did you have any luck with the Magic Search? If you found at least seven of the 13 items, you've got potential!

The Witch Wiz Quiz

How much do you already know about being a witch or a wizard? You may have read a lot of books on the subject, or seen a lot of movies. What you know already will help you with this quiz, but what you can figure out is even more important. This is a multiple choice test, so look at all the answers and then try to pick the very best one. As you think about the questions, try to imagine how a wizard would answer them. And when you're finished, the answers will be waiting for you. But don't peek! That will just ruin your fun.

WORDS to KNOW

trait: a distinguishing quality such as "curiosity" or "imagination"

potion: something a witch or wizard brews to make something happen

1. Which would usually not be helpful to a wizard?
    o. A cat
    r. A troll
    c. An owl
    f. A fairy
2. What is the most important **trait** a wizard can have?
    o. Imagination
    v. Curiosity
    x. Stick-to-itive-ness
    r. All of the above
3. If you wanted to brew a **potion** and discovered you were out of one of the ingredients, what would you do?
    b. Get mad
    t. Wait, and brew another day
    i. Figure out what you could use as a substitute for the ingredient
    z. Invent a whole new potion

what did the big witch say to the little witch?

WORDS to KNOW

crystal ball: one of many ways witches and wizards use to look into the future

4. What's the best way to deal with a dragon?
   w. Outsmart them
   f. Run
   y. Call the fire department
   n. There's no such thing as a dragon

5. What is transfiguration?
   o. The bus system wizards use
   g. Something that helps you with math problems
   i. A form of magic that turns something into something else
   q. Where wizards go to lose weight

6. If you are mixing up a potion to attract a Valentine, what would you not use?
   l. Cinnamon hearts
   b. White chocolate chips
   j. Rose petals
   d. Warts

7. Spells work best if they:
   q. Rhyme
   c. Are short
   w. Ask for something specific
   z. All of the above

8. What would you not find in a wizard's closet?
   p. A hat in the shape of a cone
   d. Bug spray
   j. A magic wand
   y. A purple robe

9. What is *your* most magical day of the year?
   l. Mugwump Day
   h. Old Wizards' Eve
   u. Unicorn Sunday
   z. Your birthday

10. What is not a way of predicting the future?
    g. Gazing into a **crystal ball**
    i. Guessing
    t. Reading cookie crumbs
    v. Astrology

11. How many toes does a three-toed toad have?
    z. Twelve
    k. Two
    i. Three
    z. Seven

Presto Change-o

How many animals or fantastic creatures can you find hiding in the word TRANSFIGURATION? We predict you can find at least five. Write your answers on the lines provided. Remember, you can use each letter only one time.

_____   _____   _____

_____   _____   _____

_____   _____   _____

_____   _____   _____

_____   _____   _____

_____   _____   _____

Reading Is Magical

Ella Enchanted by Gail Carson Levine
When a foolish fairy bestows upon Ella the gift of "obedience" at her birth, the child must always do whatever anyone tells her to do. As she searches for a way to break the curse, Ella uses her intelligence, fiesty nature, and good humor to deal with the complications that arise. A refreshing version of the Cinderella story, it was a Newbery honor book.

12. What is Green Magic?
    - c.   The kind of magic Irish wizards use
    - m.   What you use to make money magically appear
    - a.   The kind of magic that uses things you grow
    - h.   The kind of magic that helps you turn bullies green
13. Where can you find magic?
    - a.   In a smile
    - a.   In a rainbow
    - a.   In a story
    - a.   In your heart

So . . . did you have trouble? Or was this quiz a cinch? Look at the letters that represent your answers. Are any of them W, I, Z, A, R, or D? Are all of them? If you can spell "w-i-z-a-r-d" when you unscramble your answers, then you definitely have magical potential!

Chapter 2

Magical Clothing and Accessories

Part of the fun in wanting to be magical, is trying to look like your favorite witches and wizards. Can you see yourself in a long, flowing robe with a tall, cone-shaped hat on your head? Would you like to make your own special wand to create your own special magic? Would it be handy to have a magic pouch in which to carry magical objects, or a broomstick to shoo away a bad mood? If so, then this chapter will have you dressed like a witch or a wizard in no time!

Robes

Traditionally, wizards wore floor-length robes, made of velvet or silk that were heavily decorated with magical symbols. You don't need special material to make your own robe. You can make one out of a sheet, towel, or blanket. Just wrap the fabric over your shoulders and fasten it in the front with a safety pin. Your mother may even have a neat brooch or other piece of jewelry she may let you borrow to hold your robe in place.

Witches and wizards feel it is very important to consider the meanings behind the colors they choose to wear. Are you full of energy when you wear your red shirt? Do you feel more creative in your yellow sweater? Different colors can represent different qualities and feelings. You may want to consider this when choosing the color for your robe.

Magical Tip

Be sure to ask a parent for permission first before using anything around your house.

A Robe Filled With Magic

How many of these magical symbols can you find on the wizard's robe and hat?

7
book of magic
broom
carrot
cat
cauldron
cloud
crystal ball
daisy
dolphin
dragon
ladybug
Leo the Lion
moon
quill pen
rainbow
sand
spider
stars
strawberry
sun
tea cup
the knight
unicorn
VII

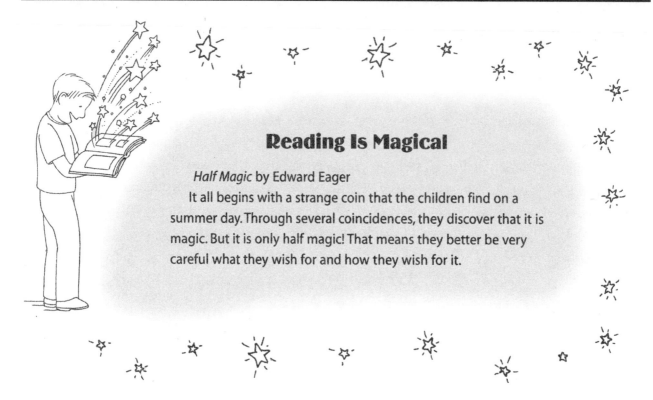

Reading Is Magical

Half Magic by Edward Eager

It all begins with a strange coin that the children find on a summer day. Through several coincidences, they discover that it is magic. But it is only half magic! That means they better be very careful what they wish for and how they wish for it.

Which of the following colors do you think describes you best?

Purple: Leadership, Wisdom

Are you always in charge? A purple robe might suit you.

Pink: Love, Friendship

Are you a true friend? A pink robe might be perfect for you.

Blue: Loyalty, Honesty

Are you loyal and trustworthy? A blue robe might be best
for you.

Red: Strength, Energy

Are you strong and full of energy? A red robe might work
well for you.

Yellow: Creativity, Joy

Are you musical or artistic? A yellow robe might be just the
one for you.

Orange: Happiness, Positive Thinking
Are you usually happy? An orange robe might be exactly you.
Green: Growth, Luck
Do you like to learn new things? Are you always lucky?
    A green robe might be grand for you.
Brown: Calming
Do you worry a lot? A brown robe might be your best bet.
White: Anything, Everything, New Beginnings
Do you like to try new things? A white robe might be the
    thing for you.
Black: Protection
Feeling scared? A black robe may be just what you need.

You can decorate your robe with stars, moons, cats, or any other magic symbols that you like. Cut them out of paper or cloth and pin or sew them on wherever you want them. If you can't make a robe, don't worry. You don't have to have a robe to feel like a witch or a wizard. Just wear your everyday clothes in your favorite colors and feel the magic inside you!

Hats

When we think of witches and wizards, we picture them wearing tall, pointed hats. Would you like to make an easy one of your own to wear when you're feeling magical?

You will need a large piece of construction paper (12″ x 18″) and some tape. Pick a color of paper that suits you best. You might want your hat to match your robe, or you may choose a contrasting color. You might pick a color for its magical quality, or you may decide on a color just because you like that color. Whatever color you pick is great. It is your hat!

FUN FACT

Charms and Tokens

Centuries ago, magic-makers used natural substances like stones or bones, which they sometimes carved into shapes of animals or symbols. These charms and tokens, which where supposed to have magical powers, would then be made into jewelry, sewn onto their clothing, or slipped into their pouches or pockets.

FUN FACT

"Bubble, bubble, toil and trouble..."

Many of the pictures we see of witches and wizards show them stirring something in a black iron pot called a cauldron. Centuries ago, magic-makers couldn't afford a lot of bowls and pots. Usually, they had to use one size to brew whatever they needed. A large container made from a material that could be placed over an open fire was a very good choice.

Lay the construction paper on a flat surface in front of you. Take the top two corners and lift them toward you and toward each other. They will form a cone. Tape the cone shut.

Your hat can stay a solid color, or you can decorate it. Maybe you'd like to draw some magical symbols on it. Maybe you'd like to jazz it up with stickers or ribbons. Be creative—and make the hat uniquely yours.

Wands

A magic wand is the most important tool for a witch or a wizard. Through it they can direct all of their magic. Most children's books and movies show wands as fairly plain sticks, but *your* wand can reflect your own interests, style, and creativity. You can decorate it any way you want.

But first you need a branch. Look for a small branch or stick that has fallen off a tree. DO NOT break one off yourself! You do not want to hurt the tree. Find one on the ground that feels natural in your hand.

Decide on a source of light for the tip of your wand. This might be a star made from shiny material, an eraser covered with glitter, or yellow paint. Anything that represents light will work. Attach your choice to the end of the stick—and you have a wand!

You may want to cover the length of your wand with one or more colors. You could add a rainbow of ribbons or smother the whole thing with stickers. Use your imagination to make your very own special wand. And maybe you'll want more than one! Witches and wizards can have as many as they want.

Hold your wand in the hand that is most comfortable for you. For instance, if you are right-handed, you'll probably want to hold it in your right hand. Hold it firmly, but not too tightly. Let

Which Wand Is Which?

Can you help this poor little witch? She's made Magic Wands in almost every color. Now she can't remember which wand to use with each of the following empowerment spells:

Star-filled wand of deepest _____, show me what is loyal and true.

Bold _____ wand, give me strength today, and help me chase mischief-makers away!

Little _____ wand, so cheerful and pretty, bring me a friend who is smart and witty!

_____ wand, made from vine and tree, bring luck and prosperity home to me.

Bright _____ wand, filled with glee, bring me joy and creativity!

Magic wand of _____ bright, lead me to wisdom and insight.

it be a natural part of you. It should be as easy as holding a pencil or a hairbrush.

How do you fill your wand with magic? That's easy. Remember . . . you are full of magical potential. Just close your eyes and picture all your magical powers charging through your body like sparkling stars. Your wand will be filled with magic.

If it is a sunny day, you can try charging your wand with the sun. Close your eyes, point your wand up toward the sun, and say these words:

Swirling stars and blinding light,
Empower my wand with all your might!

Magical Tip

DO NOT look at the sun when you try this. You could hurt your eyes!

Broom

The witch's broom was originally created to ward off, or "sweep away," evil spirits. Since most were made from the broom plant, they were called broomsticks. Magic-makers also started using them during their magical celebrations, sometimes riding them like hobbyhorses. That's where the idea of witches riding high on broomsticks comes from.

Would you like to make your own magic broom? As with your wand, you need to find the materials outside. Gather a bunch of wispy stalks or twigs. Bind them to a longer stick with string or a rubber band. Decorate your broom with your favorite colors and magical symbols.

Mischief makers, silly and gay, Brighten someone else's day.

Anytime you want to "sweep" something out of your life, use your magic broom! For example, if you can't seem to shake a bad mood, try this activity. First, close all the doors leading to other rooms in the house. Then open all the doors and windows leading to the outside. Grab your broom and, starting in one corner, sweep three times toward an open window or door, saying:

Doom and gloom,
Begone from this room!

Repeat this saying in each corner of the room. Place your broom back in the corner where you began. Close each of the open windows and doors while, with strength and confidence, you say:

And stay out!

WORDS to KNOW

magic pouch: a bag that stores the ingredients you need to make your magic

Magic Pouch

A **magic pouch** is a drawstring bag for carrying and storing magical things. Traditionally, these pouches were made out of leather or cloth, something light yet sturdy. They were decorated with magic symbols, beads, feathers, seeds, fur, or bits of colorful cord. Some were the size of a bag of marbles for small tokens, while others were larger for carrying bigger objects.

If you would like to make a magic pouch, you can do so fairly easily. You will need a bandana, a needle with a large eyehole, and 36 inches of embroidery floss. Thread the needle with the floss. Pull the end all the way down and knot both ends together at the bottom so that you have double-strength thread.

Magical Tip

If you need a really big magic pouch, you might use a pillowcase, shopping sack, or even your backpack!

Reading Is Magical

Hidden Stairs and the Magic Carpet by Tony Abbott
The first book in the Secret of Droon series, about a parallel universe entered through the basement where the struggle between good and evil is laid out in a fantasy world.

Lay the bandana on a flat surface. Starting at one corner, sew great big stitches (about an inch apart) around the bandana. Have the knot from the thread on the outside and try to stay about a half an inch down from the hem. As you sew, the material will bunch up, and when you get all the way back to where you started, you will have a medium-sized pouch.

You should have extra thread at the end. Knot it as far from the material as you can so that you can open and close your pouch. If you want to get fancy, you can add beads to the thread near the knots as "pulls," or add other decorations.

INTENT FOCUS DESIRE

Chapter 3

Magical Things

Magical Tip

You may want to color-code your Book of Magic by using colored paper that matches your moods and emotions. For example, write love or friendship spells on pink paper!

Now that you've tested your magical potential and are dressed like a witch or a wizard, you probably want to try practicing some magic. But before we get to that step, it might be smart to take the time to get organized. In this chapter, you can design your own Book of Magic. You can also read about planning Magic Minutes and creating a Magic Wish List. And you may even learn how to create **Spells**!

Book of Magic

Your Book of Magic is a very special object. In it you can keep all of your notes, drawings, and other keepsakes from your interest in magic. Maybe you created a poem about witches. Maybe you have a photograph of your best friend in a wizard costume. Maybe you drew a wonderful picture of a unicorn. All of these things can go in your Book of Magic. It is your personal magic scrapbook and journal.

WORDS to KNOW

spells: recipes that when used make specific things happen

Making Your Book of Magic

A plain, three-ring binder photograph album works well for a Book of Magic. Use the kind that lets you peel back the clear cover on each page, rather than the kind where you slide pictures into plastic pockets. The three-ring design allows you to add blank paper or move pages of notes, stories, and drawings easily.

And with the photo pages, you can collect cards, pictures, and other keepsakes.

Decorate the cover of your Book of Magic with your favorite magic symbols. You can draw them in glitter glue or sparkle paint, or attach synthetic gemstones, beads, feathers, ribbons, dried **herbs** or flowers, pictures, or photos. Like your wand, your Book of Magic is a reflection of your own creativity!

Use your Book of Magic as a place to store everything associated with your interest in magic. In years to come, you'll be able to look back and see all the fun things you did.

Magic Itches

Where You Feel It	What to Expect
On the top of your head	A wonderful surprise
In your right ear	Compliments
In your left ear	Hurtful gossip
On your nose	To be kissed by a fool
On your right palm	Money
On your left palm	An unexpected expense
On your tummy	An invitation
On your right foot	A profitable journey
On your left foot	An unprofitable journey

Magic Minutes

When you are in the mood to be magical, plan for some Magic Minutes. These are minutes you can take all to yourself, with no distractions. You may find these Magic Minutes when you first wake up in the morning, after school, after dinner, on the weekend, or in the evening. During this time, open your mind to all sights, sounds, smells, textures, or tastes and, most important, your feelings. During these Magic Minutes, you just might see or sense a magical sign.

Witches and wizards have been reading signs since time began. An *omen*, which is a sign or indication, could be something you see or something you feel. It can be either good or bad. In fact, the same omen can mean something good in one part of the world, and something bad in another. For example, if you're in Great Britain and a black cat crosses your path, it's

WORDS to KNOW

herbs: plants valued for their medicinal qualities

Good and Bad Luck Omens

Good Luck Omens	Bad Luck Omens
A four-leaf clover	Opening an umbrella indoors
A ladybug	Putting a hat on the bed
A white butterfly	Putting shoes on a chair or table
A horseshoe	Putting your left shoe on first
A wishbone	Giving away a present
A black cat entering your house	Buttoning your shirt wrong
A strange dog following you home	A cat leaving home unexpectedly
A spider crossing a wall	A picture falling
Crickets singing	An owl hooting three times
Waking up, facing south	Getting out of bed, left foot first
Putting your dress on inside out	Putting your shirt on inside out
Picking up a penny	Dropping a glove
Sneezing three times before breakfast	Complaining before breakfast

a sign for you to expect good luck. However, if you're in the United States, it's a sign of bad luck.

Magic Wish List

A Magic Wish List can help you keep track of your wishes or the goals you want to accomplish. Write your wish list in your Magic Book. You can have one main wish or several wishes. Your wishes can range from things like "I wish I had some chocolate ice cream right now!" to "I wish I could find my baseball glove" to "I wish I could be a fantastic artist." There are no right or wrong wishes. Be sure to keep your wish list where you'll see it every day—and where you can add to it easily!

Today Is Your Lucky Day

Look at the following group of omens. Cross out all the bad omens using a black or red marker. Circle all the good luck omens with a green marker, and color them green for extra luck.

Reading Is Magical

Bed-Knobs and Broomsticks by Mary Norton
Three children go on a number of exciting trips with the help of an
aspiring witch.

Chronicles of Narnia by C. S. Lewis
This seven-book series tells the history of a fantastic world called Narnia.
When four children step through the back of a wardrobe, they enter a place
of enchanted creatures where the battle between good and evil is constant.

During your Magical Minutes, you can think about your
wishes. You might come up with some terrific ideas on ways to
help make those wishes come true.

Magical Words

There are many magical words that go along with witches and
wizards. A *spell* is a form of words believed to have magical
power. Spells do not have to rhyme, but they certainly are
easier to remember if they do—and they are lots of fun to
make up! A one- or two-line spell is simple to create and

If You Wish

Using a white gel pen, or white crayon, connect the numbered stars
to find out what this witch is wishing for.

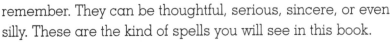
remember. They can be thoughtful, serious, sincere, or even silly. These are the kind of spells you will see in this book.

To *cast* a spell just means to say it out loud. You "put it forth" and hope that what you say comes true. Sometimes it does, and sometimes it doesn't.

Before you try to make up your own spells, see if you can fill in the missing words in both of these:

Birthday wish, now I make,
Let chocolate fudge cover my _____.
   or
Wild lavender, growing willy-nilly,
Bring me a friend who's smart and _____.

Creating and Casting Spells

Did you guess the words "cake" and "silly" in the those two spells? If you did, you're ready to create a spell or two of your own.

What you'll need:
Your Wish List

Best time to create:
Anytime

How to create:
1. Find some Magic Minutes
2. Choose one item on your Wish List. Write it here:

3. Think of words that go with your wish. Focus on how your wish looks, smells, feels, sounds, or tastes. Write some of those words here:

Picture the Details

This wizard's studio is jam-packed with magic tools. Look at this picture carefully. Try to absorb every detail. Then turn the page, picture the wizard's studio in your mind, and write down as many details as you can remember. Can you list 13 magic objects? Try for 26!

Reading Is Magical

The Hobbit by J. R. R. Tolkien
Bilbo Baggins, a hobbit (or little person), sets off on a hazardous adventure to help reclaim a stolen fortune from a dragon.

4. Try making up short sentences about your wish. Can you think of words that rhyme with the last word in your sentence? If not, change the words around or come up with a new sentence. Write a possible sentence here:

5. Play with the words until you have two short sentences that make sense about your wish. Write your newly created spell here:

6. Try casting your spell by saying the words out loud. Do you like the way it sounds? Can you see a picture of it in your mind? Focus on the wish while you say the words.

Chapter 4

Art and Music Magic

Now you're probably ready to try a little magic. Do you like to draw pictures? Do you like to write stories? Do you like to sing or play a musical instrument? If so, this chapter may be perfect for you. It includes Picture Magic for the artists, Word Magic for the writers, and Rhythm and Rhyme Magic for the musicians. On top of that, there is **Collage** Magic for very special wishes, as well as Ribbon and Cord Magic and Magic Bead Weaves for any crafty kids out there.

Picture Magic

Artwork is a wonderful way to express your emotions. Through your drawings, you can show others how you feel, what you want, and how you look at the world. When you draw, others can appreciate your own unique talents.

What you'll need:
Your Wish List
Drawing tablet
Pencil, pen, crayons, colored pencils, or markers

When to do it:
Anytime

What to do:
1. Find time for some Magic Minutes.
2. Choose one item on your Wish List.

3. Make up your own spell, or say these words while drawing a picture of what you want:.

> Magic words and pictures dear,
> Help my special wish draw near.

4. If your wish involves something positive, display the paper or keep it in a special place. If your wish involves a problem, tear the paper into tiny pieces and bury it or throw it away.

Don't worry if your drawing isn't perfect. And don't compare your artwork to someone else's. That isn't fair to you—or them. Be happy with your own creation. And if you don't want to share it with anyone else, you certainly don't have to.

Word Magic

There is definitely power in words. Ask any writer. Your special word magic may be in writing stories or in keeping a journal or diary. Believe it or not, even book reports can be magical if they bring you good grades!

What you'll need:
Your Wish List
Journal, diary, or Magic Book
Pen or pencil

When to do it:
Anytime

What to do:
1. Find time for some Magic Minutes.
2. Choose one item on your Wish List.

3. Write a short story or a diary entry describing you *having* what you want. Make up your own spell, or say these words:

> Magic words I hold so dear,
> Help my special wish draw near.

4. As with picture magic, if a positive wish is involved, display the paper or put it in a special place. If it is a negative wish, rip up the paper and bury it, or throw the pieces away.

Magical Tip

Match the color of paper or ink you use with the intent of your wish. For example, use purple for a wish involving wisdom or leadership.

Words, like artwork, are personal. Share them if you like, or keep them private in your Book of Magic. One of the best things about words is that they can always be changed. If you think of a better way to say something, write it again. Most good writers know that their words do not come out perfectly the first time around!

Collage Magic

This is a great activity for your most special wishes. It will take a bit of time and effort, but it will be worth it. You don't have to make this collage in one sitting. Add to it a little at a time or whenever you come across something that will be perfect for it. Part of the fun is watching the collage change and grow as you move closer to your wish coming true!

What you'll need:
Magazines, newspapers, postcards
Scissors
Glue
Poster board

Best time to do it:

Daytime

What to do:

1. Choose one special wish for your Magic Collage. Start collecting pictures that represent that wish. For example, if you really want to travel, start finding pictures of the places you want to visit. You can also gather words that have to do with your wish. If you want to go to Florida, you might cut out words like "sunny" or "oranges." Find all the words and pictures you can, even though you may not use them all. That way you'll have a lot to choose from in making your collage.

2. Glue the clippings to your poster board. Put the largest pieces down first and use the small ones to overlap. Make sure to let all the important parts show.

Hang your collage in your room or someplace where you can see it often. Try to think of practical ways you can help make that wish come true. Talk to your friends and your parents. This will show them how important this particular wish is to you, and they may have ideas on ways to help make it come true.

Magical Tip

Corkboard makes a nice alternative to poster board. Use pushpins instead of glue to attach your words and pictures. The best part of making the collage this way is that you can change parts of it whenever you desire.

Witch Wit

When is it bad luck for a black cat to follow you?

When you're a mouse!

Rhythm and Rhyme Magic

Music can be magical. It is a universal language that can be enjoyed by everyone. If you like singing or playing an instrument, you're a natural for Rhythm and Rhyme Magic.

What you'll need:
Your Wish List
An instrument

When to do it:
When you won't disturb anyone

What to do:
1. Find time for some Magic Minutes.
2. Choose one item from your Wish List, and select an instrument. Your voice can be your instrument if you like to sing.
3. Make up your own spell, or say these words over your instrument:

> *Rhythm and Rhyme, come together as one,*
> *Let the beat carry my wish, along with the fun.*

Type of Wish	Instrument
Protection/Beginnings	Bell
Energy/Communication	Drum
Love/Friendship	Chimes or xylophone
Joy/Happiness	Flute or recorder
Wisdom/Psychic powers	Harmonica
Success/Leadership	Keyboard
Learning/Exploring	Stringed instrument

FUN FACT

Bells and drums are favorite instruments for witches and wizards. Try ringing a bell before you cast your spells, or beating out the rhythm of your spells on a drum.

Some people believe you can add extra power to your Rhythm and Rhyme Magic by choosing an instrument that matches the intent of your wish.

4. Think of a song you like. Change the words to describe your wish. (It doesn't matter what the song is about. You could change "Twinkle, Twinkle, Little Star" into a wish about patching up a quarrel with a friend.)
5. Put your wish to music!

If you have friends that sing or play instruments, invite them over and do this activity together. This will double the magic—and the fun!

Magical Tip

To practice an advanced form of Rhythm and Rhyme Magic, try coming up with your own words *and* music!

Ribbon and Cord Magic

Do you like to do crafts with your hands? Does the wish you desire bear repeating? If you like to braid or tie knots, Ribbon and Cord Magic may be the right activity for you.

What you'll need:
Your Wish List
Colored ribbon or cord
Scissors
Yardstick
Lap-size corkboard and push pins, or clipboard

When to do it:
Anytime

What to do:
1. Find time for some Magic Minutes.
2. Choose one item from your Wish List and a color (or colors) of ribbon or cord that matches the intent of your wish.

FUN FACT

You can't play a wind instrument and sing at the same time. If you play a flute, harmonica, saxophone, or other instrument where you need to blow, alternate playing the instrument and singing when you do your music magic.

3. Make up your own spell, or say these words over your ribbon or cord:

> Colors bright, like petals on a flower,
> Weave my wish in your magic power.

4. Using your scissors and yardstick, cut three strands of ribbon or cord that are each 13 inches long.
5. Knot the strands together at the top, and pin the knot to your corkboard or clamp it on your clipboard.
6. State what you want as you braid or knot your ribbon or cord 13 times. If you've chosen to braid it, tie three knots at the end to hold your braid in place.

Twisted Magic

Oops, these two magic, makers have gotten their cord charms knotted together! Using two different colors, follow the wizard's and the witch's cord to the center. Can you predict who will get the charmed bead?

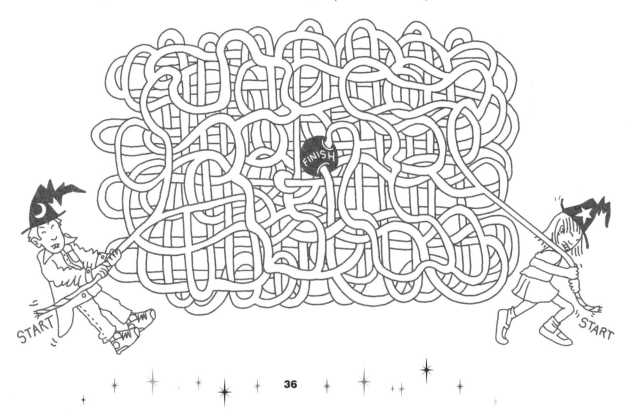

7. If your wish is something positive, keep your magic weave. If it involves a problem, bury it or throw it away.

If you were wishing for something for another person, you might want to give that person the ribbon or cord weave when you are done.

Magic Bead Weaves

Is there someone you'd like to give a special magical present? These Magic Bead Weaves can be attached to a key ring, used as a bookmark, threaded through a Magic Pouch, tied around a wrist or ankle, or even glued onto a pet's collar. This way, those you care about can carry your good wishes with them wherever they go.

Materials:
Yardstick
Colored (1/8 inch wide) ribbon or cord
Scissors
Corkboard and push pins, or clipboard
9 small colored beads

Directions:
1. Using your scissors and yardstick, cut one strand of ribbon or cord that is 26 inches long. Then cut one strand of ribbon or cord that is 13 inches long.

Color Magic

Choose your color of ribbon or cord by the type of wish you have:

Type of Wish	Ribbon or Cord Color
Leadership/Wisdom	Purple
Love/Friendship	Pink
Favors/Kindness	Lavender
Loyalty/Honesty/Dreams	Blue
Strength/Protection	Red
Communication/Creativity/Joy	Yellow
Motivation/Happiness	Orange
Growth/Prosperity/Luck	Green
Decisions/Change	Teal (Blue-Green)
Grounding/Calming	Brown
Victory/Success	Gold
Solving Mysteries	Silver
Anything/Beginnings	White
Protection/Banishment	Black

Magical Tip

To make your weave feel more magical, glue a piece of purple felt over the surface of your corkboard or clipboard.

(continued)

FUN FACT

The color of your ribbon or cord and beads should coordinate with the intent of your good wishes. Also, your spell should be short and sweet. It should say exactly what you want the bead to do. For example, if you're making a weave for your grandma to help ease her arthritis pain, your spell should sound something like this:

Tiny white bead, like snow so pure, for Grandma's pain, begin a cure.

2. Fold the 26-inch strand in half. Leaving a 1-inch loop, knot it together with the 13-inch strand, as shown. P in the knot to your corkboard or clamp it on your clipboard.

3. To braid, cross the left strand over the center strand, and then the right strand over the center strand. Repeat this five times (so you have six weaves in all).

4. Create a short spell to go with your wish. Cast it on one of the beads as you thread it through the center strand. Push the bead up to the braid, as far as it will go. Cross the left strand over the center strand, then the right strand over the center strand. Repeat this two times, adding three beads in all. Remember to repeat the spell for each bead you add.

5. Cross left over center, then right over center, nine times.

6. Add three more beads.

7. Braid nine more times.

8. Add the final three beads.

9. Add six final weaves.

10. Knot all three strands together. Tie a small knot at the end of each strand.

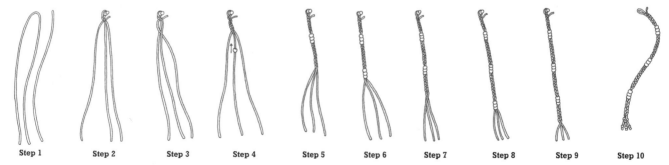

| Step 1 | Step 2 | Step 3 | Step 4 | Step 5 | Step 6 | Step 7 | Step 8 | Step 9 | Step 10 |

Chapter 5

Plant and Food Magic

Plants, all by themselves, are pretty magical things. You start with tiny seeds and in a very short time, you have beautiful plants and flowers. If you like gardening (or Green Magic), then the activities in this chapter should have special appeal. You can plant a Magic Garden or make a Magic Bouquet. You can taste some Food Magic or create Sugar and Spice Witch Bottles.

Mis-spelling Spell

Oops! Seems like the fairies have gotten into this witch's cupboard and rearranged the letters on her bottles of magic plants. Can you undo the fairies' mischief and correctly spell the name on each label? Perhaps you should use a red pencil to keep those mischief-makers away!

VROCEL
_ _ _ _ _ _

SERSO
_ _ _ _ _

CILAL
_ _ _ _ _

PANCIT
_ _ _ _ _ _

Magic Garden

Herbs and flowers have many magical qualities. A magical garden can be a special bed in your backyard, pots on your patio or deck, or even a simple windowsill garden. You can grow your plants from seeds, transplant seedlings grown at a nursery, or buy potted plants.

What you'll need:
Your Wish List
Your Magic Garden

When to do it:
Daytime

What to do:
1. If you're growing plants from seeds, find some Magic Minutes.

2. Choose one item on your Wish List, and match it to one type of seed.

3. Make up your own spell, or say these words over the seeds:

   Magic seeds, blossom and grow,
   So very soon, my wish I may sow.

4. Plant the seeds. Each time you water, repeat your wish. Do the same for each type of seed you're planting. As your plants grow, so will your wishes!

5. If you're transplanting or using prepotted plants, just replace the word "seeds" with the word "plant" in your chant. Then, each time you water, repeat your wish.

Remember to share in the wonder as your plants grow and bloom!

Magic Bouquet

Here's a way to bring a little magic into the life of someone you care about. Begin with fresh white carnations and then watch as with each new day, they magically fill with color!

Materials:
3 sheets of colored tissue paper
Scissors
Plastic soda or water bottle
Rubber band
3 lengths of ribbon (each 18 inches)
Pebbles or marbles
Water
7-Up
Food coloring
Fresh white carnations

Magical Tip

As a bonus, you can use what you harvest from your Magic Garden for new spells and wishes! Magic Bouquets, Magic Bundle, and Magic Potpourri are just a few magic uses!

(continued)

Green Magic

Here are some magical plants along with their most popular uses:

Herb or Flower	Type of Wish or Spell
Basil	Love, Happiness, Freedom
Carnation	Energy, Healing
Catnip	Joy, Playfulness, Insight
Chamomile	Energy, Success, Healing
Chrysanthemum	Happiness, Power, Strength
Clover	Luck, Prosperity, Mischief
Daisy	Happiness, Friendship, New Beginnings
Geranium	Protection, Attracting Familiars
Jasmine	Solving Mysteries, Attracting Love
Lavender	Love, Beauty, Kindness
Lilac	Seeing the Future, Harmony
Marigold	Awareness, Vision, Dreams
Mint	Prosperity, Healing, Adventure
Nasturtium	Success, Excitement, Creativity
Pansy	Dreams, Fairies
Periwinkle	Mischief, Riddles, Laughter
Poppy	Resourcefulness, Persistence, Adventure
Primrose	Abundance, Productivity, Dispelling Gloom
Rose	Love, Psychic Powers, Understanding
Rosemary	Protection, Healing, Learning, Success
Sage	Health, Wisdom, Understanding
Snapdragon	Protection, Courage, Strength
Sunflower	Wishes, Faithfulness, Growth, Truth
Thyme	Health, Healing, Courage, Dreams, Hope
Violets	Faithfulness, Forgiveness, Dispelling Jealousy

Directions:
1. Find time for some Magic Minutes.
2. Choose a wish for your Magic Bouquet.
3. Make up a spell, or say these words over all
   your materials:
   Ingredients of this Magic Bouquet,
   Help grow my wish, day by day.
4. Lay the colored tissue paper on a flat surface.
   Each sheet should be 2 1/2 times the length of your
   plastic bottle. Arrange the tissue so the sheets
   crisscross each other.
5. Carefully cut the top off your clean, dry bottle, where it
   begins to curve in. Place your bottle in the center of
   the tissue, and draw the tissue up around the bottle.
6. Holding the tissue at the top of the bottle, slide the
   rubber band up from the bottom of the bottle until it is
   very close to the top. Let the tissue above the rubber
   band gently fold over, like a collar.
7. Place the three ribbons around the bottle, 1 to 3 inches
   from the top, and tie them in a bow.
8. Place the pebbles or marbles in the bottom of the bottle
   (to keep it from tipping over), and carefully fill the bottle
   3/4 full of water, without getting the tissue wet.
9. Add a dash of 7-Up, and a drop or two of food coloring.
10. Clip the stem of each carnation at a slant, so it can
    drink up your magic potion!

Food Magic

We all have our favorite foods—ones we like more than any
others. When we eat these foods, we feel happy and content.
But did you ever think of eating peanut butter to cement a

FuN FACT

Choose a food coloring
that matches the theme
or intent of your wish. If
your food coloring only
comes in blue, red, and
yellow, try these
combinations to get
different colors:

Blue + Yellow = Green

Blue + Red = Purple

Yellow + Red = Orange

Pink = 1 drop of Red

friendship? Or bananas to gain courage? Or pizza to be creative? These are things to consider with food magic. Whenever you're ready for a tasty snack, maybe you should choose a food that will boost the wish you're focusing on.

What you'll need:
Your Wish List
Food!

When to do it:
Anytime

Magic Friendship Bundles

This wizard has created Magic Friendship Bundles by selecting three, six, nine, or thirteen sprigs of flowers or herbs, and tying them with a colorful ribbon or cord. But now he's forgotten which charm goes with which bundle. Can you help?

Magic Bundles

1. Nasturtiums & Basil

2. Catnip & Daisies

3. Rosemary & Sage

4. Clover & Mint

5. Roses & Lavender

6. Sunflowers & Thyme

7. Pansies & Periwinkles

Magic Charms

A. *"Bring me a love, with beauty inside,*
     Whose psychic powers reach far and wide."

B. *"Mischief and adventure, let this friend bring,*
     With luck and prosperity, fit for a king!"

C. *"Bring me a friend, who's playful and fun,*
     To explore all that's new, under the sun."

D. *"Happy and wild, creative and free,*
     Let this friend bring success to me."

E. *"With this friend I'll grow hopes and dreams,*
     And faithfully wish on magic moonbeams."

F. *"Bring me a friend, with wisdom and knowledge;*
     A study-buddy, for the road to college."

G. *"Searching for fairies, mischief, and riddles,*
     With this friend I'll laugh more than a little."

What to do:

Start by making a trip to the grocery store or the refrigerator!

1. Find time for some Magic Minutes.
2. Choose one item on your Wish List, and match it to a type of food.
3. Make up a spell, or say these words over your food:
   Glorious food, nutritious and yummy,
   Grant my wish, as you fill my tummy.
4. As you eat your magic snack, picture how you want it to help you.

If you're eating your snack with a friend or family member, you can discuss other ways to make this particular wish come true.

Mmm-Mmm-Magic

This wizard is trying to brew a magic soup. He wants better vision, wisdom, insight, extra confidence, and strength. With luck and patience, this soup will also bring him a new beginning. Can you fit the food items that he'll need into the cauldron? The salt and water are already simmering.

Food Magic

Here is a list of magical food items:

Food	Type of Wish	Food	Type of Wish
Almonds	Wisdom, Health	Meat	Strength, Victory
Apple	Health, Knowledge	Milk	Strength, Endurance
Banana	Strength, Courage	Nutmeg	Memory, Dreams
Beans	Banishing, Protection	Oats	Beauty, Abundance
Bread	Friendship, Prosperity	Oranges	Happiness, Faithfulness
Carrot	Vision, Clarity	Pasta	Endurance, Persistence
Celery	Insight, Focus	Peaches	Truth, Beauty
Cheese	Wisdom, Perspective	Peanut butter	Cementing friendships
Cherries	Learning, Friendship	Pepper	Protection, Excitement
Chocolate	Energy, Joy	Pizza	Working together, Creativity
Cinnamon	Friendship, Confidence, Protection	Potatoes	Worry, Uncertainty
Cloves	Protection, Love, Strength	Raspberries	Love, Forgiveness
Corn	Abundance, Luck	Rice	Patience, Persistence
Dill pickles	Protection, Strength	Salt	Cleansing, Banishing
Eggs	New Beginnings, Growth	Strawberries	Romance, Playfulness
Ginger	Magic, Mystery, Joy	Sugar	Sweet love, Prosperity
Grapes	Dreams, Prosperity	Vanilla	Love, Enchantment
Lettuce	Money, Health	Walnuts	Learning, Growth
Marshmallows	Joining, Melding	Water	Beauty, Cleansing

Reading Is Magical

Lost Years of Merlin by T. A. Barron
This is the first volume in a series about the younger years of
the great wizard Merlin. Suffering from amnesia, the boy
discovers his strange powers and is determined to discover his
identity.

Sugar and Spice Witch Bottles

A *potion* is a liquid mixture. For centuries, witches and wizards
traditionally created sets of "Witch Bottles" filled with colorful
magic potions. The bottles (or jars) could be any size or
shape, but they were always clear to display each potion's
bright color.

Here's a way for you to create your own Witch Bottles with
colorful sugar-crystal potions. You can find colored sugar crystals at most craft and cake decorating stores. Start by making
one, and whenever you find an interesting bottle or jar, you can
always make another!

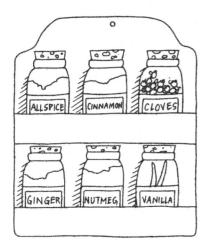

Materials:
Small bottles or jars (with tops)
Colored sugar crystals
Spices (See sidebar chart)

Directions:
1. Find time for some Magic Minutes.
2. Choose a wish for each Sugar and Spice Witch Bottle.
3. Gather the ingredients for each jar, and cast a spell as you "brew" your potion!
4. To brew, fill each jar with sugar crystals, and then sprinkle in the spice.

These make nice gifts for friends and family, especially if you include a tag that explains the meaning of the color and the spice.

Magic Potion Recipes

Potion	Sugar Color	Spice
Creativity	Yellow	Allspice
Friendship	Pink	Cinnamon
Strength	Red	Cloves
Happiness	Orange	Ginger
Dreams	Blue	Nutmeg
Enchantment	Purple	Vanilla bean

Chapter 6

Friendship Magic

There is nothing more magical than having friends. Some friends share activities like sports or music with you. Others live nearby or are in the same classes with you at school. If you're really lucky, you meet a friend who connects with you in a very special way. They become your "best" friend. Try some of these spells if you're looking for new friends—or enjoying the ones you already have.

Magical Best Friends

Would you like to find your all-time best friend in the whole world? Look in the mirror! You will always be your very best friend. To help you find other true friends, try this activity.

What you'll need:
½ Yard of pink ribbon
½ Yard of blue ribbon
½ Yard of white ribbon
Glue
Small, round mirror
Rose quartz crystals
Lavender buds
Token (optional)

When to do it:
Anytime

What to do:

1. Braid the three ribbons together. (Pink is for friendship, blue for loyalty and honesty, and white for new beginnings.)
2. Glue the braid around the outside of the mirror.
3. Place the rose quartz crystals and lavender buds (both for friendship) on the mirror, saying:

> A true blue friend, allow me to see,
> So a true, blue friend, I can be.

Magical Tip

If you have a special interest you would like your new friend to share, put a token symbolizing that interest with the crystals and lavender. For example, if you love to play soccer, put a tiny soccer ball on the mirror. Or if you like music, a charm in the shape of a musical note would be the perfect thing.

Care and Keeping of Friends

Taking care of your friends is very important. Time spent together and fun activities allow for magical memories to be created. Invite some of your favorite friends over and try this activity.

Ingredients:
Bread
Gingerbread people cookie cutters
Peanut butter
Bananas
Strawberry jam
Chocolate chips
Large plate
Napkins and drinks

(continued)

Directions:

1. Take slices of bread (for friendship and prosperity), and cut out gingerbread people.
2. Have a friend spread the bread with peanut butter (to cement your friendships).
3. Have another friend add slices of banana (to give your friendships strength and courage).
4. Another can add some strawberry jam (for playfulness and humor).
5. And another can top your friendship sandwiches with chocolate chips (for joy).
6. As each sandwich is finished, place them on one large plate, in a circle, so that each hand touches the next. When you have enough open-faced sandwiches for everyone, pass out napkins and drinks, and dig in!

Picture This

This wizard is trying very hard to picture the details of what he wants.
Can you use the combination of pictures and letters to figure out his spell?

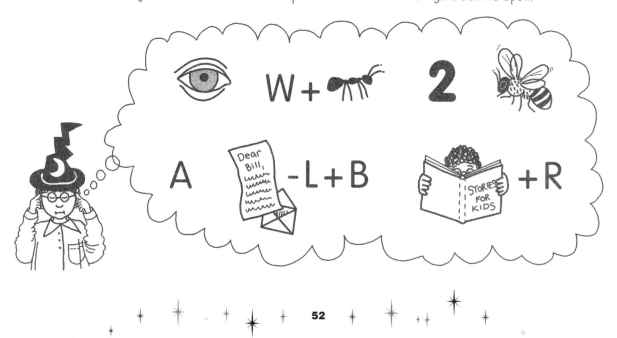

Could It Be Love?

Do all your friends have crushes at school?
Do you feel like you're the only one who
doesn't? Try this spell, and maybe you'll be
lucky to meet someone special too.

What you'll need:
Pink or red pen or pencil
4-by-6-inch piece of paper
Bud vase
Water
7-Up
White, pink, or red rose

When to do it:
Anytime

What to do:
1. Using the paper and pencil, make a Wish List of every-
    thing you would like in someone special.
2. Fill the bud vase three-fourths full with water. Add a
    dash of 7-Up (to bring you sweet love).
3. Roll your Wish List around the stem of the rose, and
    place it in the vase, saying:
    > *Rose of love, and water sweet,*
    > *A special love I want to meet.*

Of course, you can't just sit at home waiting for that
someone to come knocking on your door. Get involved at
school or in your community. Try a new activity or sport.
Do things that get you out and about, and allow you to meet
new people.

Magical Tip

If you have friends that live far away, why
not send them a surprise care package?
Everyone loves to receive a batch of their
favorite homemade cookies!

Reading Is Magical

Mary Poppins by P. L. Travers
Jane and Michael Banks have no idea the fun in store for them when Mary Poppins appears at their house. Those familiar with the movie will be happy to know that the books in this series contain many more wonderful adventures with this magical nanny.

Magical Me

If you've met someone you'd like to make your special someone, here's a potion that just might make you irresistible!

Materials:
Scissors
3-by-3-inch square of soft, white cloth
13 cinnamon hearts
13 white chocolate chips
6-inch length of red ribbon

Directions:
1. Cut little zigzags on the edges of the cloth.

2. Place the cinnamon hearts (for friendship) and the white chocolate chips (for sweet love and enchantment) in the center of the cloth.

    Bring the four corners of the cloth together and wrap the ribbon around the bundle. Tie the ribbon in a bow (not a knot) just above the hearts and chips, saying:

    > *Hearts and chips, a magnet be,*
    > *Draw _____'s attention to only me.*

4. Find your special someone, and open your magic potion nearby so he or she is sure to share some.

Magical Tip

Be extra careful not to get any water in the chocolate, because even just a drop or two will make the chocolate too thick to stir, and you'll have to start over again.

You cannot force anyone to feel things that they don't feel. If your crush is not interested in you, there are plenty of other people in the world. Keep looking and, eventually, the person you like will feel the same way toward you!

Get Happy Potion

Nobody is happy all of the time. We all have days when we feel sad and discouraged. If one of your friends is feeling unhappy or upset, try this potion as a way to help cheer them up.

Ingredients:
13 strawberries
Powdered allspice
White plate
1 cup chopped chocolate
Microwavable bowl
Microwave oven

(continued)

Witch Wit

How do you make
a witch scratch?

You make her "w" disappear!

Directions:

1. Wash the strawberries, leaving the tops on, and blot them completely dry with paper towels.
2. Sprinkle a pinch of allspice (for playfulness) in the center of the plate, then place the plate in the refrigerator (to help cool down a bad mood).
3. Place the chocolate (for joy) in a microwavable bowl. Melt the chocolate on low power for 30 seconds. Stir the chocolate. Repeat until the chocolate is melted. Dipping or coating chocolate (available in most craft and cake decorating stores) works best.
4. Take the white plate out of the refrigerator.
5. Dip each strawberry in the chocolate, saying:
   > *Magical strawberry, playful and sweet,*
   > *Help (<u>your friend's name</u>) get back on*
   > *cheerful feet.*
6. After it's dipped, place each strawberry on the cool plate. When all 13 strawberries are dipped, place the plate back in the refrigerator for thirteen minutes.
7. Share your magic strawberries with your friend.

While you are enjoying this treat, your friend may feel like talking about what is bothering them. Together you may be able to come up with other ways to help the situation.

Chapter 7

Miscellaneous Magic

Magical Tip

Try Whisper Magic while swinging in a hammock, or rocking gently in a chair. You may find yourself doing it for much longer than three minutes!

No Muss—No Fuss Magic

The following activities are very easy, but lots of fun. And the best part is that you probably already have everything you need to do them. Whisper Magic, Bubble Magic, and Hug Magic are very quiet kinds of magic. In the end, you may find that these simple types of magic are the ones you like the best!

Whisper Magic

If you like to daydream, Whisper Magic may work well for you. This form of magic requires no special tools and can be practiced anytime or anywhere.

What you'll need:
Your Wish List

When to do it:
Anytime

How to practice:
1. Find some Magic Minutes.
2. Choose one item on your Wish List.
3. Close your eyes, picture your wish, and cast a spell—*in a whisper*. For example, you might say:
    Unicorns and castles, and stars in the night,
    Bring me my wish, when the time is right.
4. Next, spend three minutes picturing yourself *having* what you want. The more detailed your image the better.

Don't expect immediate results with any type of magic. But don't give up either. Everyone is entitled to wishes, and often dreams do come true. Believe in yourself!

Bubble Magic

Bubbles floating through the air are very magical. Where do they go as they drift away? Maybe they bounce off waves in the ocean. Maybe they come to rest on pine trees in the woods. Maybe they float right past your best friend's window. You never know!

Bubble Magic is so full of possibilities that it is a very special way to send off your magical wishes. Or if you are worried about something, it is also a great way to carry your troubles away.

What you'll need:
Your Wish List
Bubble wand
Bubble solution

Mini Vision Bubble Maze

Find your way through the bubbles from the witch to the magic sign. What does the sign tell about your future?

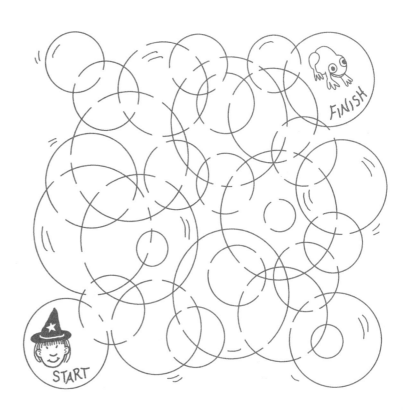

When to do it:

Daytime

What to do:

1. Find a few Magic Minutes.
2. Choose one item on your Wish List.
3. If it is a positive wish you are hoping for, stir the bubble solution three times with your bubble wand and say:

    Magic Bubbles, sail up and away,
    And bring me my wish, without delay!

    Say your wish very clearly and then blow a stream of bubbles. Now, picture the bubbles giving your wish flight, soaring high to become a reality.
4. If your wish is a worry you would like to be rid of, stir the bubble solution three times with the bubble wand and say:

    Fearless Bubbles, carry this away,
    Take my troubles with you, this very day!

Picture your problem being carried away in the bubbles—never to trouble you again!

Of course, just wishing your problems away is not very practical. It often helps to talk out your troubles with a friend, teacher, or parent. You don't have to face worries alone. There is sure to be someone to help you, no matter how bad things may seem.

Magical Tip

A bubble wand with a star-shaped tip would make Bubble Magic even more fun!

Hug Magic

This form of magic is best done with a friend. And it is a great one when celebrating something or when facing a difficult situation. Hug Magic lets you join forces with another person and share your positive energies. Hugging always feels right with the right person!

What you'll need:
Someone you care about
His or her special wish

When to do it:
Anytime

What to do:
1. Choose a special time.
2. Give your friend a hug, while saying,

    What I want most in the world right now,
    Is for you to _____.
3. Don't let go! Together you should picture your friend *having* what he or she wants. Make sure to hold that hug for at least three minutes!

More Magic Spells

This is the place to find magic of all kinds. You might want to try Grade A Potion if you have a big test coming up. Or Score! if you're facing an important game. You might see if Money Magic helps you to conjure up some funds for a special purchase. You might find the Farewell Spell helpful if a friend is moving away. Every situation can present its own type of magic. You just need to look for it!

Magical Tip

This box might be a great place to keep your Wish Lists!

Magical Wish Box

Find a small box you can use for this activity. It can be wood, ceramic, or cardboard. It doesn't matter. Decorate the box to show your own unique personality.

Then try the following:

Materials:
Sand
Small box
Multicolored star glitter
Small magnifying glass
Small globe
Small pictures/tokens (optional)

Directions:
1. Sprinkle the sand in the box, saying:
    Fill my life with Magic Minutes
2. Sprinkle in the star glitter, saying:
    And all my hopes and dreams
3. Add the magnifying glass, saying:
    Magnify my magic abilities
4. Add the small globe, saying:
    And open to me a world of possibilities
5. You may also add small pictures or tokens that represent specific things that you want now or in the future. For example, if you long for a puppy, add a picture or likeness of the one you want and, while placing it in your Magical Wish Box, say:
    Just one more wish, a special plea,
    Bring this Labrador puppy to me.

WORDS to KNOW

prism: cut glass that disperses light into its separate colors

A Rainbow of Magic

A **prism** is a solid, transparent object that can break up a ray of light into the colors of the rainbow. Hanging from a window, it can throw rainbow fragments all over your room whenever the sun shines. And with the bow may come a boost of magic power and insight.

Materials:
Prism/Crystal
Cord/String of beads

Directions:
1. Hang a crystal or prism in your window, saying:
   Rainbow of colors; red, green, and blue,
   Put a magic glow in all that I do.

Lucky 13

Witches and wizards consider the number 13 very lucky because there are 13 full moons each year. So, if you want to attract luck, maybe you should try this spell.

Materials:
Green paper
Scissors
Small pot
13-inch length of green ribbon
13 marbles
Ladybug or butterfly likeness (optional)

Magical Tip

Crystals can be expensive. Try looking at yard sales for old lamps that have prisms on them.

(continued)

Directions:

1. Cut a four-leaf clover (for luck) out of the green paper that is slightly larger than the bottom of your pot. Put it where your pot will stay.
2. Tie the green ribbon (for luck and prosperity) around the pot, near the top.
3. Place each of the thirteen marbles (for the power of 13 full moons) in the pot, saying:

    Like the moons, full with mystery and power,
    Fill my life with luck, every minute, every hour.

   This might be a particularly good activity on one of those days when everything seems to go wrong!

Grade A Potion

Tests are part of going to school. There is no getting around them. Everyone has to take them, and everyone worries at least a little bit about the results. Before your next big test, why not try this potion to get you in a "smart" mood.

Ingredients:
Applesauce
Chopped almonds
Chopped walnuts
Nutmeg
Paper
Purple pen
A sprig of sage (optional)
Purple ribbon (optional)

Directions:

1. Mix together the applesauce (for knowledge), nuts (for wisdom and learning), and a tiny pinch of nutmeg (for memory), saying:

> *Apple of knowledge, nuts so wise,*
> *Help me get the "A" I prize.*

2. As you eat your applesauce, write, "*(Your Name)*, 'A' Student," 13 times with a purple pen.
3. For extra help, tie a sprig of sage (for wisdom) with a purple ribbon (for magic wisdom) and use it as a bookmark.

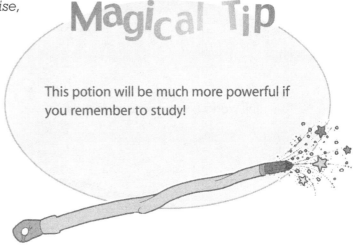

Magical Tip

This potion will be much more powerful if you remember to study!

Score!

Is there a big game or meet coming up? Are you feeling pressure to win, win, win? You can't win all the time, but you can try this potion to give your athletic abilities a little boost.

Ingredients:
Chocolate ice cream
Mashed banana
Milk
Cinnamon stick

Directions:
1. Scoop the chocolate ice cream (for energy) into a glass.
2. Add some mashed banana (for strength and courage).
3. Pour in some milk (for endurance and extra strength).
4. Stir with the cinnamon stick (for confidence), saying:

> *With this potion, and this spell,*
> *At my sport, help me excel.*

That old saying, "It's not whether you win or lose, it's how you play the game," is really true. If you've done your very best, you can be proud of yourself no matter what the outcome.

Magical Tip

This spell works best on a cloud-free day.

Creativity Booster

When you're trying to be creative, you have to let your imagination soar. Maybe the best way to do that would be be to go fly a kite! Try it—and see what happens.

Materials:
A yellow kite
Glitter paint and paintbrush
3 lengths of purple ribbon (each
         13 inches)
3 small keys or paper butterflies
String

Directions:
1. Paint moons (for creativity) on your kite.
2. When the paint is dry, attach the three strands of purple ribbon (for magical insight) to your kite.
3. On each strand of ribbon, tie a paper butterfly (for a magical change) or a key (to unlock your creative talents), saying:
    Catch the wind, dance in the sun,
    Bring creativity to me, before you're done.
4. Now, attach the string to your kite and . . . go fly your kite! See if a friend or family member can come too. It's much more fun to do things together!

Health and Happiness Garland

We all want to be happy and healthy. To attract health and happiness to your room or home, make this magic **garland** to hang on your doorknob.

Materials:
13-inch length of green ribbon
13 herbs/flowers/tokens
13 lengths of ribbon (3 inches each, all different colors)

Directions:
1. Tie 13 evenly-spaced knots in your green ribbon.
2. At each knot, tie a sprig of herb, dried or silk flowers, or fruit, or a token that represents health and happiness to you. These tokens could be pictures of your friends or family, a smiley face sticker, a shell,or some other momento from a happy time in your life. As you tie each one on, say:
     All things wonderful and wise,
     Come to me, when I open my eyes.
3. Hang your magic garland on your doorknob. Then, each morning, when you open your eyes, look for something wonderful!

WORDS to KNOW

garland: a wreath-like decoration

Try to take care of yourself by eating right, exercising, and getting enough sleep. Sometimes we get so busy that we start neglecting these important things. And always try to look on the bright side of things. Thinking positively is one of the magic keys to happiness.

Lost and Found

Did you lose your favorite green sock? Are you trying to figure out where you put your math homework? Is Mom looking for her car keys—again? Try this spell if something is lost and you need to find it.

Materials:
13-inch length of purple ribbon
Clear quartz crystal

Directions:
1. Go to the place the lost item should be.
2. Tie the purple ribbon around the wrist of your wand hand.
3. Gently press the crystal on your forehead. Close your eyes, take three deep breaths and say:
   Magic insight clear my mind,
   And lead me to what I need to find.
4. Listen to your magical insight—and look where it leads you.

Sometimes you just need to step back, take a few breaths, and let your brain remember where something might be. And if your math homework stays missing, you'll just have to do it over again!

Chapter 8

Sun, Moon, and Star Magic

The sun, the moon, and the stars have always been magical symbols. For witches and wizards they can represent everything from simple wishes to foreseeing the future. In this chapter we will look at a couple of the magical ways that the sun, moon, and stars are viewed.

Wishing on a Star

Star light, Star bright,
First star I see tonight,
I wish I may, I wish I might,
Have the wish I wish tonight.

If you've ever recited this poem, you've already practiced the most popular form of Sun, Moon, and Star Magic. You can try to add more magic to this simple rhyme by doing the following activity.

WORDS to KNOW

astrology: the study of the influence that the stars and planets are supposed to have on people and events.

zodiac: an imaginary belt of stars in the heavens.

What you'll need:
Your Wish List
Colored pens or pencils
Paper
Scissors
A night sky

When to do it:
Just before you go to bed

What to do:
1. Find time for some Magic Minutes.
2. Choose a wish from your Wish List.

3. Trace the star pattern onto your paper. *(Wishing on a Star template on page 133)*
4. Write your wish on it, and cut the star out.
5. Holding the star next to your heart, look up into the night sky, and choose a star.
6. Recite the poem, adding your wish at the end.
7. Climb into bed, put the star under your pillow, close your eyes, and picture yourself *having* what you want.

Magical Tip

Use glitter crayons or pens when you write your wish. The sparkle will make it look even more magical!

Astrology

Astrology is the study of the influence that the stars and planets are supposed to have on people and events. The word comes from two Greek words: *astro*, meaning star, and *logos*, meaning knowledge. Thousands of years ago, astrology was used to predict victories for kings and to chart successful voyages for explorers. Today, it is fun to use astrology to try and determine a person's character, potential, and compatibility.

What you'll need:
A **zodiac** chart
Birth dates
A horoscope

When to do it:
Anytime

(continued)

Magical Tip

Watch for shooting stars—they are the most magical of all!

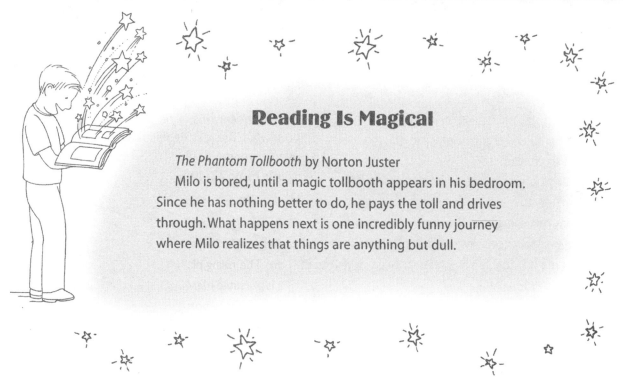

Reading Is Magical

The Phantom Tollbooth by Norton Juster
Milo is bored, until a magic tollbooth appears in his bedroom. Since he has nothing better to do, he pays the toll and drives through. What happens next is one incredibly funny journey where Milo realizes that things are anything but dull.

What to do:

1. Find your birthday, or the birth date of the person you want to know more about, on the zodiac chart. The date will fall within one of the 12 sun signs. That means, on that date, the sun was thought to have been passing through that star grouping, or constellation. Zodiac charts are all slightly different, so if a date falls at the very beginning or at the very end of one of the choices, it is said to be on the "cusp." If the date you're checking falls on the cusp, read the descriptions for both choices. You (or your friends) may fit one sun sign or the other—or maybe even both!

2. Read how the zodiac chart describes the sun sign. Most charts will tell you about the strengths and characteristics that are natural to that sign, as well as the challenges that sign will most likely face. You can also learn what other sun signs get along best with each sign.

3. To predict what the future holds for a particular sign, select a horoscope to follow. A *horoscope* is a prediction made by a person who studies astrology. The prediction is based on what the position of the stars tells the astrologer. You can find horoscopes in newspapers, magazines, books, page-a-day calendars— even on the Internet!

Zodiac Chart

Aries: March 21–April 20

Symbol: The Ram
Element: Fire
Ruling Planet: Mars
Strengths: The ruling planet, Mars, brings a competitive edge to this friendly sign. Fearless and confident, Aries is the one you want on your team! Even if they don't have the best skills, their contagious spirit will win. In love and friendship, this sign's great personality and irresistible dreams will draw you like a magnet.
Challenges: Aries can get so wound up in their own dreams, they may make hasty decisions, and their generous hearts tend to break easily.
Compatible Signs: Leo and Sagittarius

Taurus: April 21–May 21

Symbol: The Bull
Element: Earth
Ruling Planet: Venus
Strengths: Venus, the ruling planet of Taurus, brings a gentle quality to this strong, powerful sign. Those born under Taurus know what they want and are willing to

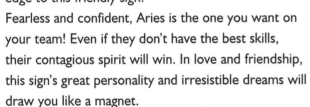

work hard to get it—no matter how long it takes! Stable and dependable, Taurus is rarely distracted or swayed. And if loyalty is what's most important to you in a friend or romance, put Taurus at the top of your list.

Challenges: Taurus can sometimes be stubborn and, sometimes, a bit possessive.
Compatible Signs: Virgo and Capricorn

Gemini: May 22–June 21

Symbol: The Twins
Element: Air
Ruling Planet: Mercury
Strengths: The ruling planet for Gemini is versatile Mercury, which makes those born under this sign talented at many things. In fact, they are at their

best when things are new or changing! Friendly and adaptable, Gemini finds it easy to talk to anyone about anything. And in love or friendship, Gemini will be agreeable, no matter what you have in mind!
Challenges: Gemini love to talk. But it can sometimes turn to gossip, and their well-intentioned plans can sometimes turn to hurtful schemes.
Compatible Signs: Libra and Aquarius

Cancer: June 22–July 23

Symbol: The Crab
Element: Water
Ruling Planet: Moon
Strengths: The mysterious moon lends a natural magnetism to this sign. Sensitive and sympathetic, Cancers have a gift for the arts and are very creative! In romance and friendship, those born under this sign

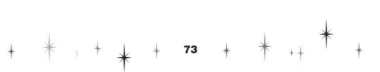

are generous with their time and heart, and bring out the best in those they love.

Challenges: Like the changing tide, sensitive Cancers can get a bit moody, and sometimes a quiet mood can be mistaken for a bad mood.

Compatible Signs: Pisces and Scorpio

Leo: July 24–August 21

Symbol: The Lion
Element: Fire
Ruling Planet: Sun
Strengths: As Leo's ruling planet, the sun shines brightly within this bold sign! Natural leaders, outgoing Leos energize those around them with their charm and confidence. In friendship and love, Leo will take ferociously good care of you.

Challenges: Sometimes Leo's energy can be a little overwhelming, and sometimes their confidence can get a little out of hand.

Compatible Signs: Aries and Sagittarius

Virgo: August 24–September 23

Symbol: The Virgin
Element: Earth
Ruling Planet: Mercury

Strengths: Versatile Mercury rules this sign. Like Gemini, this makes Virgos good at whatever they try. However, those born under this sign are more selective in what they choose to pursue. Thoughtful and careful, Virgos are quick to learn and have great memories! In love and friendship, this sign prefers one-on-one time to group activities.

Challenges: Private by nature, Virgos can sometimes seem hard to reach, and may be too thoughtful when you need a quick opinion.

Compatible Signs: Taurus and Capricorn

Libra: September 24–October 23

Symbol: The Scales
Element: Air
Ruling Planet: Venus

Strengths: This sign shares Venus as a ruling planet with Taurus. However, with Libra, Venus's gentle influence falls on a personality that strives for a balance between hard work and relaxation, giving both great importance. Libra usually finds a way to get along with everyone! And in love and friendship, Libra will always find time to play.

Challenges: Libra can sometimes appear too gentle, which can be mistaken for a lack of interest. Trying to keep everything in balance can sometimes lead to making fickle decisions.

Compatible Signs: Gemini and Aquarius

Scorpio: October 24–November 22

Symbol: The Scorpion
Element: Water
Ruling Planet: Pluto
Strengths: Pluto, the ruling planet of Scorpio, brings a lot of intensity to this sign. Passionate about whatever they think and do, Scorpio lives life to the fullest and enjoys every minute! In love and friendship, Scorpio will awaken your interests, and show you life as you've never seen it before.
Challenges: Scorpio's intensity can sometimes lead to suspicion and jealousy.
Compatible Signs: Cancer and Pisces

Sagittarius: November 23–December 21

Symbol: The Archer
Element: Fire
Ruling Planet: Jupiter
Strengths: As the ruling planet, optimistic Jupiter brings enthusiasm to the hearts of Sagittarius! Playful, broadminded, and easy-going, those born under this sign rarely take anything too seriously, but are honest and earnest in pursuing their goals. In love and friendship, this Archer's playfulness will capture your heart.
Challenges: Sometimes it would be nice for Sagittarius to take some things more seriously.
Compatible Signs: Aries and Leo

Capricorn: December 22–January 20

Symbol: The Goat
Element: Earth
Ruling Planet: Saturn
Strengths: Capricorn's ruling planet, Saturn, gives the gift of persistence. Those born under this sign are not likely to give up on their goals, and are therefore likely to be very successful. Organized and responsible, Capricorns know how to get things done! In friendship and romance, Capricorns are very thoughtful.
Challenges: Capricorns may get a little too serious from time to time.
Compatible Signs: Taurus and Virgo

Aquarius: January 21–February 19

Symbol: Water Carrier
Element: Air
Ruling Planet: Uranus
Strengths: Originality is what the ruling planet of this sign brings. Those born under Aquarius are one-of-a-kind, independent, and never fail to come up with great ideas! Resourceful and unselfish, this sign likes to help others. And in friendship and love, depend on Aquarius to be very kind.
Challenges: At times, Aquarius can be unclear, or may say what you want to hear, rather than what they really feel.
Compatible Signs: Gemini and Libra

Pisces: February 20–March 20

Symbol: The Fish

Element: Water

Ruling Planet: Neptune

Strengths: Neptune, the ruling planet for Pisces, is the master of insight and intuition. This skill lets Pisces see what's really going on, making those born under this sign very good at solving problems and knowing the right thing to say. When it comes to love and friendship, Pisces will make it fun and easy for you to swim by their side.

Challenges: Sometimes Pisces can be a little too mysterious. Some can tend to choose what will make everyone happy, rather than what is best, to keep the waters calm.

Compatible Signs: Cancer and Scorpio

Chapter 9

Predicting the Future

Would you like to know what is going to happen tomorrow? Lots of people would. Witches and wizards have been known to try many means of looking into the future—astrology, crystal balls, even tarot cards. In this chapter, you can try fun activities like Bubble Vision, Cookie Crumb Predictions, Reading Palms, and Numerology. Let's see if any of them work for you. Only time will tell!

FUN FACT

What Do the Signs Mean?

For every witch and wizard, the trickiest part of predicting the future is figuring out what the magic sign is telling you. The first thing that pops into your mind might be the likeliest choice. It could be your magical instinct talking to you.

Bubble Vision!

What you'll need:
Soap or bubble bath
Water

When to do it:
When you're washing the dishes or taking a bath

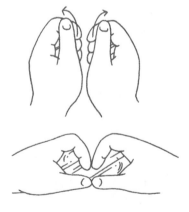

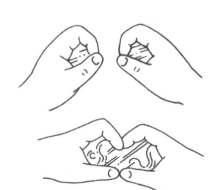

What to do:

1. Mix the soap or bubble bath with water. While getting both of your hands really soapy, ask a question about the future.
2. Make two fists, wrapping your thumbs around the outside of your index fingers. Make sure your thumbs face each other.
3. Slowly, open your fists so your index fingers trace the backs of your thumbs. Don't lose contact. There should be soap film in the circles formed by your thumbs and index fingers. (If not, start again. You may need to use a little more soap, or to go more slowly.)
4. Bring the two circles together so that the tips of your index fingers and the tips of your thumbs join.
5. *Slowly*, keeping the tips of your index fingers together, and the tips of your thumbs together, move your thumbs away from your index fingers. That will create one large transparent soap circle from the two smaller circles. (Don't feel bad if it takes several tries. This is a pretty tricky skill.)
6. Once you have one large circle, or Vision Bubble, look for a picture or magic sign in it!

Magical Tip

Not every bubble will have a sign in it. So, if at first you don't succeed, try, try again. You'll certainly get nice and clean in the process!

Magic Signs

Picture	Meaning
Cat	Be on your guard.
Crown	Victory will be yours.
Frog	Time to make a change.
Heart	Love or friendship is near.
Key	Open the door to a new opportunity.
Mask	Things are not as they seem.
Moon	Success will be elusive.
Rainbow	Prosperity is on the way.
Ship	You'll begin an adventure.
Star	Your wish will be granted.
Sun	Prospects are strong.
Unicorn	Expect a wonderful surprise.
Witch's Hat	Learn more, before you take action.

Magical Tip

Use chocolate cookies when you have a light-colored teacup. When you use a dark-colored teacup, use vanilla cookies!

Cookie Crumb Predictions

Of all the ways to predict the future, this is by far the tastiest! Some adults enjoy reading tea leaves to try and predict the future. Kids prefer reading cookie crumbs! It works the same way, but is definitely yummier!

What you'll need:

A teacup
Milk
3 cookies
A small plate
A paper napkin

When to do it:

After school, or after dinner

What to do:

1. Fill the teacup with milk.
2. If you want to predict the future for a friend, ask them to dip the cookies in the milk and eat them, while the two of you talk about what your friend wants to know. If you're doing a reading for yourself, use this time to think about what you want to know.
3. Ask your friend to drink *almost* all the milk. You want to leave just enough milk to be able to swirl the crumbs around in the cup while saying:
    Cookie crumbs, sweet and true
    Help me see what to do.
4. Cover the plate with the paper napkin. Have your friend place the cup upside down on the plate, while asking what she or he wants to know.
5. Turn the cup over and read the future!

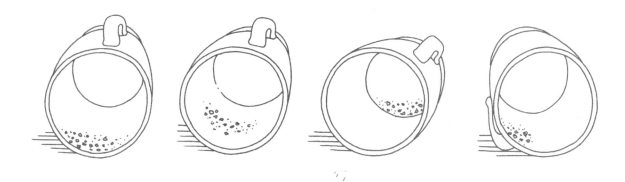

Where are most of the crumbs?

Placement	Meaning
Close to the rim of the cup	Events will happen soon.
Midcup	Events will happen in a few months.
Near the bottom of the cup	Events may not happen for six to 12 months.
Near the handle of the cup	Events will occur close to home.

Reading Palms

Palmistry is the art of reading a person's character or future from the markings on his palms. Some witches and wizards truly believe that your hands tell what your future holds. This may or may not be true, but it certainly might be fun to try it. So grab a friend and see if there is anything interesting you can predict about each other.

What you'll need:
Both hands

When to do it:
Anytime

What to do:

1. If you're reading hands for friends, determine if they are right-handed or left-handed. If they're right-handed, their *left* hand will tell you what characteristics and potential they were born with. Their *right* hand will tell you what they've experienced in life, and what their future holds. If they're left-handed, it is the opposite.

2. Take your friend's hand in yours. Turning the hand palm-side up, look at the size of the fingers in relation to the palm. If both the fingers and the palm are short, your friend may be fun-loving and likes to help others. If the fingers are longer than the palm, your friend may be very organized and responsible. A long palm with long fingers tells you they're curious and inventive. And a long palm with short fingers is your clue to someone who likes to have fun.

3. Look at where the fingers attach to the palm. If they form a straight line, success in life will come easily to this person. If there is a slight curve (which is the most common), your friend may have a very eventful, exciting life with lots of challenges and opportunities.

4. Focus on the palm, where you will see four major lines: the life line, the fate line, the heart line, and the head line.

   The future is in the palm of your hand.

Brain Power

To decipher this spell, figure out where to put each of the scrambled letters. They all fit in spaces under their own column. When you have correctly filled in the grid, you will have a good spell to boost your brain power and creativity.

	O	A	R		I							O	H			
M	M	K	R		M	R		B			O		H			
P	B	O	O	S	E	C	M	L	Y	A	T	D	E			
S	R	U	E	T	T	E	T	B	R	E	I	N	I	R		S
H	A	A	C	T	L	Y	A	Y	R	P	A	W	E	N		G

Magic Project

Cut a piece of heavy yellow paper 8½ inches long by 3 inches wide. Use an orange marker to write the Brain Power Spell on the strip of paper. Make a hole in one end of the paper, and thread through a thin purple ribbon. Tie three knots in the ribbon, and repeat the spell three times. Now, use your Brain Power Spell as a bookmark, and use the back of the bookmark to keep track of the books you have read. As the list grows longer, you can watch your brain power increase!

Life Line

Your life line runs vertically down your palm. It is the line closest to your thumb and tells the story of your energy and health.

Here's how to read your life line:

What It Looks Like	**What It Tells You**
Begins close to your index finger	You have lots of energy and ambition.
Begins at your head line	You have an even flow of energy, great stamina, and persistence.
Begins below your head line	Your energy comes in spurts as you bounce from one opportunity to the next.
Long and clear	You are naturally healthy.
Short with breaks	You need to exercise and take your vitamins.

Fate Line

Your fate line is the other vertical line. It usually runs down the center of your palm. This line will tell you your destiny.

Here's how to read your fate line:

What It Looks Like

Begins close to your index finger

Begins close to your middle finger

Begins close to your ring finger

Curves away from your life line

Joins your life line

Crosses your life line

What It Tells You

You will achieve great success at a young age.

Your life will exceed your dreams, so dream big!

You will be popular and talented.

You will travel extensively.

You will be very independent.

You will have lots of good friends and a close, loving family.

Heart Line

Your heart line is at the base of your fingers. It runs horizontally across your palm. It will tell you how you behave in love and friendship.

Here's how to read your heart line:

What It Looks Like

Very close to your fingers

Some distance from your fingers

Clear, deep, and straight

Slightly curved, with tiny breaks

Longer than your head line

What It Tells You

You are loyal and care deeply.

You are friendly and kind.

You are reserved and sincere.

You are fun and flirtatious.

Your heart rules your head.

Head Line

Why do you think the way you do? The horizontal line under your heart line reveals how you make decisions.

Here's how to read your head line:

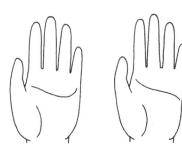    

What It Looks Like	**What It Tells You**
Curves up toward your little finger	You are realistic and practical.
Curves away from your little finger	You are creative and imaginative.
Fairly straight	You use both imagination and common sense.
Does not touch heart line	You are enthusiastic and you bounce back from difficulties.
Joins heart line	You are careful and considerate.
Crosses heart line	You are sensitive and insightful.

Numerology

Do you have a magic number? Of course you do! In fact, we all have two! One is tied to our date of birth, and one is tied to our name. **Numerology** is the study of the hidden significance of numbers. The study of numerology dates back to ancient Babylonia, but even today, it is still fun to consider.

What you'll need:
A numerology chart
Paper
Pencil

When to do it:
Anytime

What to do:
To find your Magic Birth Number:
1. Write down your birth date in number form. For example, January 19, 1993, would be 1/19/1993.
2. Add the numbers together: $1 + 1 + 9 + 1 + 9 + 9 + 3 = 33$. If the total has more than one number in it, add those two numbers together, so you end up with one number between 1 and 9. For example, $3 + 3 = 6$. Six would be your Magic Birth Number!
3. Consult a numerology chart to see what the future holds!

To find your Magic Name Number:
1. Write down the numbers that correspond to the letters in your full name.
2. Add the numbers together, as you did with your magic birth date.
3. See what the numerology chart has to say!

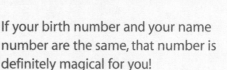

Magical Tip

If your birth number and your name number are the same, that number is definitely magical for you!

Magical Numbers Chart

This chart will help you convert your name to a number!

1 2 3 4 5 6 7 8 9
A B C D E F G H I
J K L M N O P Q R
S T U V W X Y Z

For example, if your name is Kelly Marie Zachary:

K E L L Y
2 +5 +3 +3 +7 +
M A R I E
4 +1 +9 +9 +5 +
Z A C H A R Y
8 +1 +3 +8 +1 +9 +7 = 85
  8 + 5 = 13   1 + 3 = 4
Your Magic Name Number is 4!

Number 1:

Magic Quality: Powerful Leadership
Magic Symbol: The Sun
Magic Day: Sunday
Magic Careers: Entrepreneur, Company President, Politician

You are innovative, courageous and creative. You love learning new things and solving mysteries. Your strength and confidence inspire others to embrace your ideas, and follow your lead. In love and friendship, you're the one who takes the first step and makes the plans. You get along best with 2s.

Number 2:

Magic Quality: Mysterious Wisdom
Magic Symbol: The Moon
Magic Day: Monday
Magic Careers: Judge, Psychologist, Musician

You are a gentle spirit, mysterious and artistic. Your dreams are important to you and you don't share them with many. Your charm and wisdom attract others like a magnet. In love and friendship, you're kind and understanding, and harmonize well with 1s.

Number 3:

Magic Quality: Enriching Energy
Magic Symbol: Jupiter
Magic Day: Thursday

Magic Careers: Teacher, Chef, Marketing Professional
You are a visionary, talented and disciplined. You love coming up with new ideas and seeing them spring to life. Others are attracted by your energy and independence. In love and friendship, you're generous and mix well with 6s, 9s, and other 3s.

Number 4:

Magic Quality: Internal Strength
Magic Symbol: Uranus
Magic Day: Sunday
Magic Careers: Financial Planner, Contractor, Engineer
You are a rock, stable and dependable. You love accomplishing your goals and helping others accomplish theirs. You are attracted to others for who they are, not for what they have. In love and friendship, you're loyal and reliable to a chosen few 1s, 2s, 7s, and 8s.

Number 5:

Magic Quality: Daring Resourcefulness
Magic Symbol: Mercury
Magic Day: Wednesday
Magic Careers: Astronaut, Day Trader, Spy
You are an adventurer, bright and impulsive. You love a challenge—the bigger, the better. Others are attracted to your unpredictability and your ability to bounce back from disappointments. In love and friendship, you take risks and get along well with all numbers, particularly other 5s.

Number 6:

Magic Quality: Romantic Vision
Magic Symbol: Venus
Magic Day: Friday
Magic Careers: Resort Developer, Movie Producer, Coach
You are a dream weaver, romantic and sincere. You love making dreams come true, especially those of your family and friends. Your internal beauty inspires and attracts others. In love and friendship, you're thoughtful and giving, and partner well with all numbers.

Number 7:

Magic Quality: Restless Creativity
Magic Symbol: Neptune
Magic Day: Monday
Magic Careers: Writer, Architect, Fashion or Software Designer
You are an artist, intuitive and creative. You love the process of creating, more than the pride of completion. Others are attracted to your original ideas and philosophies. In love and friendship, you're sensitive and understanding. You are most compatible with 6s and 4s.

Witch Wit

If the new kid in your class was a wizard, what would be his best subject?

Spelling!

Number 8:

Magic Quality: Intense Ambition
Magic Symbol: Saturn
Magic Day: Saturday
Magic Careers: Actor, Stockbroker, Professional Athlete
You are a star, rebellious and tenacious. (You don't give up!) You love challenging the way things are, and questioning authority. Your energy and intensity attracts others. In love and friendship, you're a whirlwind of feelings, and are understood best by 2s and 4s.

Number 9:

Magic Quality: Fierce Determination
Magic Symbol: Mars
Magic Day: Tuesday
Magic Careers: Firefighter, Attorney, Doctor
You are a fighter, strong and brave. You love coming to the rescue of others, and beating overwhelming odds. Your determination in overcoming obstacles attracts others. In love and friendship, you're protective and passionate, matching well with 3s.

Chapter 10

Animal Magic

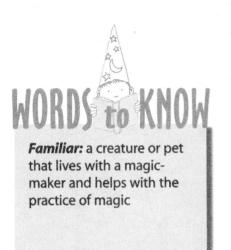

WORDS to KNOW

Familiar: a creature or pet that lives with a magic-maker and helps with the practice of magic

Animals have long been associated with magic. Some people say that animals that live with witches and wizards and help them practice magic are actually witches in disguise. Or they may be the spirit of a witch in the body of an animal, like the character Salem, in *Sabrina, the Teenage Witch*. When a creature or pet lives with a magic-maker and helps with the practice of magic, it is known as a ***Familiar***. The word "Familiar" comes from the Latin word *famulus*, which means *attendant*.

Here are some popular Familiars.

Cats

Whenever you see a witch, you know a cat can't be far behind. In fact, one legend tells us that witches can actually transform themselves into cats nine times during their lives. This may have led to the belief that cats have nine lives!

This legend may have grown out of mythology. Many goddesses associated with magic were said to have taken the shape of a cat. In Egypt, Bast, the goddess of sorcery, music, dance, and joy, preferred to be seen as a sleek feline. Hecate, the Greek goddess of the moon, and hostess of gatherings where witches and wizards exchanged secrets, would sometimes transform herself into a cat to escape danger. In China, the goddess of eternal youth and magic, Chin Mu, was also known as the cat woman. And in a Norse myth, any cat that pulled the chariot of the goddess Freyja for seven years earned the right to become a witch.

Cat Signs

How can your cat help you? It can't talk to you in words, but maybe it can communicate with you in other ways. Here is a list of what your cat just might be telling you through its behavior:

If You See a Cat:	It's a Sign You Should:
Pouncing	Pounce on a new opportunity
Sharpening its claws	Prepare for a challenge
Jumping down	Be confident (Whatever is troubling you, you're sure to land on all fours.)
Jumping up	Be confident (No goal is too high, no dream is too big.)
Playing	Take time to play
Stretching	Spend time learning something new
Meowing	Voice your opinion
Napping in the sun	Take quiet time to recharge your batteries
Backing away	Back away

Magical Tip

Carrying the image of a cat is thought to protect you from all bad luck and evil.

You Look Familiar

With a black pencil, fill in the magic triangles to discover a familiar friend.

Cat Decisions

Wouldn't it be great if your cat could help you make decisions? Try the following activity whenever you find yourself in doubt.

What you'll need:
Your cat
A decision that can be answered with a "Yes" or a "No"

When to do it:
Anytime

What to do:
1. Picture your question in your mind.
2. Call your cat.
3. Notice which paw crosses into the room first. If the right paw leads, the answer is yes. If the left paw touches down first, the answer is no.

Dogs

Although dogs are not pictured with witches and wizards as often as cats, these Familiars are thought to have more psychic sensitivity than cats. In fact, many of the goddesses who could change themselves into cats actually chose dogs to be their Familiars. Many gods and goddesses chose dogs as their companions or protectors. And, in ancient Babylon, Gula, the goddess of fate, used the symbol of a dog for magical healing.

Dog Signs

Have you ever wondered what your dog might be telling you? Here is a list of some of the possibilities:

If You See a Dog:	It's a Sign You Should:
Following a scent	Look beneath the surface
Burying a bone	Resolve a problem that's been bothering you
Scratching an ear	Rethink your strategy
Wagging its tail	You're on the right track
Yawning	Give your brain a breather
Standing on its two back legs	Try harder; what you want is almost within your reach.
Cocking its head	Expect to get a great idea
Rolling on its back	Be open to other opinions
Offering its paw	Expect to meet a new friend

Dog Decisions

Dogs may also be able to help you make decisions. Try this activity if you're looking for some canine advice.

What you'll need:
Your dog
A decision you need to make

When to do it:
Anytime

What to do:
Look your dog in the eyes while asking the question you want answered.

If your dog barks or comes toward you wagging his or her tail, the answer is yes. If your dog remains silent, grumbles, growls, or comes toward you without wagging her or his tail, the answer is no.

Owls

The wide-eyed, all-seeing owl has been a popular choice of Familiar for magic-makers since the beginning of time. In fact, the Roman word *strix* means both owl and witch. In medieval times, owls were thought to be witches in disguise and were known as *night hags*.

Owls are not practical pets for most people—but they make wonderful magical messengers in the Harry Potter books!

If you would like to decorate your room with paper bag owls, then try this activity:

Materials:
Small brown paper lunch bags
Construction paper (in different colors)
Scissors
Glue
Markers or crayons

Directions:
1. The paper bag is the body of each owl. The flap is its face. Cut out eyes, beak, feet, and feathers from construction paper. Use whatever colors suit you best.
2. Glue the owl pieces onto the bag in the appropriate places.
3. Add finishing touches with crayon or markers.
4. Place the owl (or owls) in a special spot in your room. For instance, you can slide it onto one of your bedposts if you have that sort of bed.

Magical Tip

If you rescue an animal, you will have a magical connection!

Frogs and Toads

Traditionally, frogs are a symbol of rebirth or transformation. Ancient lore tells us Hecate, the moon goddess and patron of magic, was fond of frogs.

In the Middle Ages, many of the European names used for the witch goddess Hecate also meant toad. This was not a sign of disrespect for Hecate, but rather an acknowledgment of the magical powers this amphibian was thought to have.

Witch Wit

Two witches went on a picnic, but had to wait for the third witch to show up before they could eat. Can you guess the name of the third witch?

Sandwich! (Sand-witch)

Like owls, frogs and toads are not practical pets. It is best to leave them in their natural habitat. However, there is no reason you can't go looking for them. Try this activity if you're in the mood for a nature walk:

What you'll need:
Walking shoes
A wish from your Wish List
A friend or parent
Woods or pond area

When to do it:
Daytime (during the summer is best!)

What to do:
1. Walk quietly in a wooded or pond area. Stop frequently and look carefully for frogs and toads.
2. If you see any, softly say these words:
   Frog or Toad in nature free,
   Bring my special wish to me.
3. Don't try to pick them up or bring them home. Let them hop or swim off with your wish.

Hummingbirds

Hummingbirds are not traditional Familiars, but they certainly could make great magical messengers. If you have a hummingbird feeder at home, this might be a great activity for you.

What you'll need:
A hummingbird feeder
Hummingbird nectar
Your Wish List

Reading Is Magical

Which Witch by Eva Ibbotson
Arriman the Awful holds a contest to decide which witch he should marry. Will it be Belladonna, the white witch, or one of the other local witches? Read this wonderfully clever book to find out!

When to do it:
Daytime

What to do:
1. Make a wish out loud as you fill your hummingbird feeder with sweet nectar.
2. Hang the feeder and watch as these magical creatures draw your wish from the feeder, and carry it away.

Familiar Friends

If you already have a pet, you can use this spell to turn your pet into a Familiar Friend. If you don't have a pet, you can turn one of your stuffed animals into a magical helper!

Magic Animal Signs

If you see any of the following creatures, they may be a magical sign.

Creature	Magic Message
Ant	Use your energy and determination.
Bear	Your strength and stamina will increase.
Bees	Prosperity will come to you.
Bull	Know when to be aggressive.
Butterfly	There will be a magical change in your life.
Cat	Your psychic wisdom will increase.
Cow	Expect a feeling of contentment.
Deer	Your grace and speed will increase.
Dog	A new companion will come into your life.
Dolphin	Your life will fall into a magical rhythm.
Donkey	You're being too stubborn.
Dove	Peace and love will enter your life.
Eagle	You will be able to see the bigger picture.
Elephant	An obstacle will be removed from your life.
Frog	There will be a positive change in your life.
Goat (black)	Hidden treasure is nearby.
Hawk	You will see things more clearly.
Hedgehog	Lighten up; you're being too serious.
Horse	You will have a safe journey.

Magic Animal Signs (continued)

Creature	Magic Message
Hummingbird	Happiness and joy will flitter into your life.
Monkey	Stop fooling around.
Mouse	Watch for deception.
Otter	You will find a hidden talent.
Owl	You will gain special knowledge.
Parrot	Be careful of repeating rumors or gossip.
Peacock	Let people see how beautiful you are.
Quail	If you scurry, victory will be yours.
Rabbit	Your intuition will grow stronger.
Raccoon	Now is a good time to be curious.
Robin	You will make a new start.
Seal	You will be protected from hurtful rumors.
Sheep	You will have to navigate a tricky path.
Spider	You will have a creative inspiration.
Squirrel	It's time to prepare for the future.
Swan	You will be able to see into the future.
Turkey	A gift is on the way.
Turtle	It's time to slow your pace and enjoy life.
Whale	Your psychic powers will increase.

Abracadabra

What do you think of when you hear the word "ABRACADABRA"? A magician pulling a rabbit out of a hat? A puff of smoke and someone disappearing? Well, a long time ago, abracadabra was used as a power word to get rid of sickness. In those days, magic-makers would write the word 11 times in a triangle, each time leaving one letter off the word. When the word had "disappeared", the illness was supposed to be gone, too! To see how one of these magic charms might have looked, fill in the blanks in this triangle. Decorate your charm using the colors for energy, strength, luck and protection.

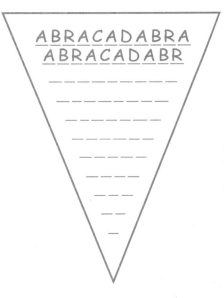

What you'll need:
3 pet treats (cookies for stuffed animals)
Purple dish
A plastic frog or a picture of a frog (optional)
Magic Wand
Your pet or stuffed animal

When to do it:
Anytime

What to do:
1. Place the treats (or cookies) on the purple dish (purple attracts magic power).
2. To increase the power of your spell, place a plastic frog (or a picture of a frog) on the dish as well. Frogs help transform things.
3. Imagine all the magic power within you swirling around like a galaxy of stars. Wave your Magic Wand over the treats. Imagine those stars of magic shooting out of your wand, covering the treats, as you say:

    Into pills of magic, turn these treats,
    So (your pet's name or stuffed animal's name)
    Can help me with magical feats.

4. Feed the treats to your pet. (If you're using a stuffed animal, you get to eat the cookies!)

Take particularly good care of your Familiar—especially if it is a real pet. Remember to feed it and show it lots of affection. Both cats and dogs generally love to be petted. And most dogs can't wait to go for a nice, long walk.

Chapter 11

A Calendar of Magic:
Halloween to the Spring Equinox

Magical calendars are filled with celebrations! Each minute of the day contains a special magic. So does each day of the week, each week of the month, each month of the year, and every year of your life. The trick is to celebrate each and every moment.

Magic New Year: October 31

Also known as Halloween, this is the most important festival for witches and wizards. Magic-makers use this time to celebrate the spirits of loved ones who have gone on to their next life. On this one magical night, they believe that these spirits return to give them help and guidance. These spirits are not fierce or scary. They are kind and loving. If you have a gathering at your house next Halloween, you might want to try some Calling-All-Friendly-Spirits Cider or make some Ghostbuster Balls. You might even want to play a round of Playing Favorites.

Calling-All-Friendly-Spirits Cider

You'll be able to serve three people with this fruit-and-spice cider.

Ingredients:
1 cup apple cider
1 cup cherry juice
1 cup grape juice
9 whole cloves
9 whole allspice
3 cinnamon bark sticks

Witch Wit

Try this tough tongue twister: Wendy Witch was weaving wishes. Which wish was Wendy weaving? Wendy was weaving wristwatch wishes!

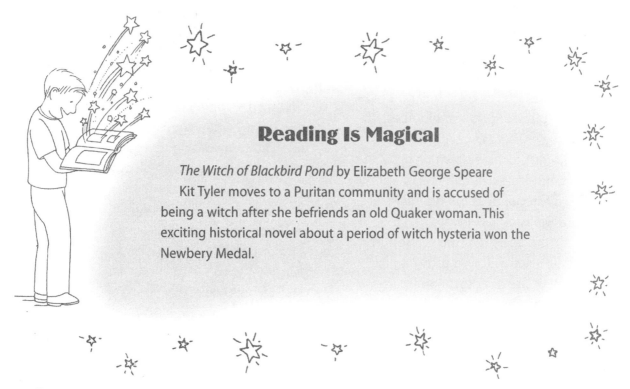

Reading Is Magical

The Witch of Blackbird Pond by Elizabeth George Speare
Kit Tyler moves to a Puritan community and is accused of being a witch after she befriends an old Quaker woman. This exciting historical novel about a period of witch hysteria won the Newbery Medal.

Directions:

1. Place all ingredients, except the cinnamon sticks, in a covered pot, and bring to a gentle simmer over low heat.
2. Turn the stove off and, keeping the lid on the pot, let it stand for 30 minutes.
3. Remove the cloves and allspice. Pour the cider into a mug, and add a cinnamon stick!

This might be the perfect drink for when you come back from Trick-or-Treating—especially if it is a chilly night!

Ghostbuster Balls

Are you afraid of ghosts? Well, ghosts are not supposed to like the smell of cloves. So, if you and your friends want to try and keep ghosts away, then maybe you should try making these spicy fruit balls.

Materials:
¼ cup whole cloves
A fresh, ripe tangerine
1 yard of ¼-inch ribbon
Glue

(continued)

Directions:
1. Press the cloves into the tangerine, covering the tangerine.
2. Cut the length of ribbon in half. Find the center point of each half and glue the two pieces of ribbon together so that they crisscross perpendicularly.
3. Lay the ribbon face down on a flat surface, and draw a 3-inch line of glue on each strand of ribbon, beginning where the ribbons cross.
4. Center the bottom of the tangerine on the crisscross, and draw two opposing strands of ribbon up and around the tangerine (so the tangerine is divided in half). Join the strands at the top with a knot.
5. Draw the remaining two strands up and around the tangerine (so the tangerine is now divided into quarters). Join the second two strands at the top with a knot.
6. Knot all four ribbon strands together at the base, and again, leaving a 1-inch loop.

Hang the ghostbuster balls in your house. If nothing else, they will make it smell really good!

Playing Favorites

How well do you really know the members of your family? Do you know Dad's favorite movie? Or Mom's favorite song? How about Grandma's favorite color? This is a great game to play when you have a family gathering. If you pay attention, you'll probably pick up a lot of fun facts about all of your relatives!

Materials:
A Playing Favorites list
Pen or pencil
Basket
Pad or notebook
Tape recorder (optional)
Camera (optional)

Sample List:

Favorite keepsake	Favorite toy
Favorite book	Favorite family story
Favorite song	Favorite piece of advice
Favorite movie	Favorite joke
Favorite smell	Favorite flower
Favorite treat	Favorite flavor
Favorite fruit	Favorite vegetable
Favorite sport	Favorite hobby
Favorite animal	Favorite friend
Favorite memory	

Directions:

1. Invite relatives from your grandparents' generation, from your parents' generation, and from your generation to gather and play. You need at least one person from each generation, but the more the merrier!

2. Make a Playing Favorites list. You can use all or part of the one shown here, or create your own. Write each item in question form. Then, cut out each question, fold it up, and place it in the basket.

3. When your guests arrive, have them gather in a circle. If you have a tape recorder, turn it on. (Sometimes it's fun, after the game, to play back some of the answers.) And, if you have a camera, be sure to take pictures throughout the game.

4. Choose one relative to be your first Star, and another to keep track of who wins points.

5. Pass the basket around, having everyone, except your Star, choose one question. Eyes closed, please!

6. Starting to the right of your Star, have the person unfold the slip of paper and guess your Star's favorite _____(whatever is written on the paper).

7. If the answer is right, the person gets a point! If not, two more relatives can take a guess to win a point, before the Star reveals the answer.

8. When everyone in the circle has had a turn, the current Star gets to pick the next Star. Each rela-

Magic Hink Pinks

The answer to each Hink Pink is two rhyming words with the same number of syllables. For once the fairies are being helpful—they left you some letters as hints!

1. An Irish enchantress who specializes in charms about water.

   — — U I —   — — U I —

2. A male magic-maker who specializes in creating big snow storms.
   — — — Z Z — — —   — — Z — — —

3. A female spell-caster who sews all her charms with a needle and thread.
   — — I T — —   — I T — —

tive gets to be a Star once during the game. When the new Star is chosen, place all the slips of paper back in the basket and begin again.

9. When everyone has gotten a chance to be a Star, tally up the points!

If you play this game throughout the year on different holidays, you'll get better and better at it every time.

Winter Solstice: December 20–22

The Winter Solstice is often called the shortest day of the year. From this date forward, the days begin to lengthen, and people celebrate the return of the sun. To encourage the return of a fruitful summer, some witches and wizards hang ornaments of fruits, nuts, seeds, and berries on the branches of outdoor trees. This makes them very popular with the local birds! They may also place wishes on the branches of a Yule tree. If you're in a holiday wishing kind of mood, you may want to try the Magical Wish S'Mores, make a Secret Wish Tree, or throw a Beckoning Tree Party.

Magical Wish S'Mores

These are called Magical Wish S'Mores because, when you taste them, you'll wish you had some more! You also get to tuck three special wishes into each sweet snack.

Ingredients:
Maraschino cherries
Large marshmallows
Graham crackers
Chocolate bars

Directions:
1. Preheat your oven to 350 degrees. Line a cookie sheet with foil.
2. Take the stems off the maraschino cherries, slice each one in half, and place the halves on a paper towel to drain.
3. Cut each large marshmallow in half, lengthwise.
4. Layer a square of graham cracker with a smaller square of chocolate, three maraschino cherry halves—*making a wish on each cherry*—and two marshmallow halves.
5. Place the Magical Wish S'Mores on the cookie sheet. Bake them, for 5 minutes, or until the marshmallow begins to melt.
6. Let the S'Mores cool for a few minutes, so you don't burn the roof of your mouth!

Secret Wish Tree

This is fantastic way to send lots of wishes to all your friends and family. There is no limit on wishes. You can send as many as you want, as often as you want.

Materials:
Paper
Pens or pencils
Ruler
Scissors
1/8-inch-wide ribbon or cord
Small hole punch
A Wish Tree

Directions:
1. Cut the paper into 3-by-3-inch squares, or larger, if you like.
2. Think of a wish for someone you care about, and write it on one of the squares.
3. Fold the square in quarters. Punch a hole in the only corner that does not have a fold.
4. Cut a 6-inch length of ribbon. Thread the ribbon through the hole, and tie one knot near the hole, and two more where the ends of the ribbon meet. Say your wish aloud as you tie each knot. (If others can hear, *think* your wish, so it remains a secret for the time being.)
5. Write the name of the person for whom the wish is intended on the outside of the folded square.
6. Place the wish on your Secret Wish Tree! If your family has a Christmas tree, you may want to make that your Secret Wish Tree. If not, it's best to use an artificial tree, or a small living tree that you can transplant into your garden. (Your Secret Wish Tree doesn't have to be an evergreen.)
7. Select a special time (perhaps New Year's Eve) to open and share, or deliver, wishes!

Make extra squares of paper and invite others to make wishes! You can even turn it into a party. Remember, if others are present,

Magical Tip

Secret Wish Trees make excellent gifts for special people. Give a Secret Wish Tree complete with secret wishes, or with instructions and all the materials so the recipient can create her or his own Secret Wish Tree.

Powerful Wishes

To increase the magical power of your wishes, coordinate the color of paper or ink, and ribbon or cord, with the intent of the wish.

Purple:
Leadership/Wisdom

Pink:
Love/Friendship

Blue:
Loyalty/Dreams

Red:
Strength/Energy

Yellow:
Creativity/Joy

Orange:
Motivation/Happiness

Green:
Growth/Prosperity

Brown:
Grounding/Calming

White:
Anything/Everything/
New Beginnings

have everyone *think* of their wishes as they're tying the knots, so all wishes remain secret until you have an Opening Party.

Beckoning Tree Party

During this festival, many magic-makers invite friends over to decorate outside trees with fruit, nut, or seed ornaments, to beckon the return of the fruits of Summer. As a bonus, this magical tree will attract many grateful birds!

When you invite your friends to your Beckoning Tree Party, be sure to ask them to bring edible ornaments for the wild birds. You can find edible ornaments in the pet section of most stores. Or, you can make your own with this easy recipe.

Materials:
Wax paper
¼ cup margarine
40 large marshmallows
5 cups of any combination of the following:
 seeds, nuts, dried fruit bits, cereal, birdfeed
Cookie cutters
Small nail
Colorful ribbon, string, or cord

Directions:
1. Cover a flat surface with two 2-foot strips of wax paper. Tape the two strips together. Place heavy books on either end of the paper to hold it in place.
2. Melt the margarine and marshmallows in a large pot, over a low heat, stirring constantly.
3. When all the marshmallows are melted, remove from heat and add the 5 cups of edibles. Work quickly!
4. Pour the mixture onto the wax paper. Spread to an even ½-inch thickness.

5. When completely cool, cut the mixture into shapes with cookie cutters. Using a small nail, press a hole approximately ½ inch from the top, and add a 6-inch length of ribbon or cord. Tie a knot at the top of the ornament and two more where the two ends of the ribbon meet.

You may also want to make garlands out of popcorn and cranberries. First, measure a 6-foot length of thread. Then, thread a needle. Tie the two ends of the thread together, making a 3-foot length. Finally, string the popped popcorn and cranberries! The birds will love the garlands as well.

Festival of Light: February 2

This festival celebrates what witches and wizards consider to be the first day of Spring, when the frozen earth begins to thaw. Another name for this festival is Candlemas, because many feel lighting candles helps the sun rekindle its full, nurturing warmth. It is a creative time when you could whip up some Candlelight Brownies, make a Magical Scrapbook for a friend, or spin a Magic, Never-Ending Tale.

Candlelight Brownies

As the flicker of candles light the night during this festival, sweet white chocolate chips light up these rich, chewy brownies! This delicious recipe makes 4 giant or 16 bite-size brownies.

Ingredients:
½ cup butter
½ cup + 1 tablespoon flour
4 ounces semisweet chocolate
¼ teaspoon salt
2 tablespoons cocoa powder
3 eggs
½ cup granulated sugar
¼ cup dark brown sugar
1 teaspoon vanilla
1 cup white chocolate chips

Directions:
1. Preheat your oven to 350 degrees. Lightly butter an 8-inch square baking pan. Dust with 1 tablespoon of flour.
2. Melt the semisweet chocolate and remaining butter in the top of a double boiler, over hot (not boiling) water. Stir constantly until smooth. Remove from the heat and cool to room temperature.
3. Sift together the remaining flour, salt, and cocoa powder. Set aside.
4. Beat together the eggs, sugars, and vanilla.

(continued)

5. Fold the egg mixture into the cooled chocolate mixture.
6. Fold in the flour mixture, ¼ cup at a time.
7. Add the white chocolate chips, saving some to sprinkle on top.
8. Spread into the prepared pan. Sprinkle the remaining chips on top. Bake for 25 to 30 minutes. Cool completely (on a wire rack) before cutting.

You can also use your favorite packaged brownie mix. Just add 1 cup of white chocolate chips!

A Magical Scrapbook

If you have already made yourself a Book of Magic, you may want to create something similar for someone you care about. Your family and friends can use it to keep photographs, cards, letters, keepsakes—anything that brings the magic of love and memories into their lives.

Materials:
1 plain-cover, 3-ring-binder-style photo album or scrapbook (The kind where the pages peel back for photos, rather than the kind that has plastic pockets for photos)
Glitter-ink pens
Construction paper
Hole punch

Optional: Synthetic gemstones, glitter glue, sequins, beads, dried flowers, dried herbs, ribbon, photos, pictures, glue

Directions:
1. Decorate the cover of the Scrapbook in your own creative style. Use any or all of the items suggested, or use items your own imagination conjures up.
2. If you're making the book for a friend who is also interested in magic, you can add decorated pages of construction paper with favorite spells, potions, charms, or activities.
3. If you're making the book for a friend who is not interested in magic, add decorated pages with favorite stories, poems, quotes, jokes, recipes, or pictures.
4. Be sure to add extra pages of construction paper with decorated borders for future notes, thoughts, and ideas.

Magic, Never-Ending Tale

This is a time rich with creative inspiration, so gather your friends and spin a web of magical tales. First, you'll need a Magic Theme List. Actually, the list can have any theme, but the Festival of Light is a good time to play with a theme related to magic. You can make a list of all the magical words you like or, you can make a specific list. For example, you could write down things from your favorite book with a magical theme (names of characters, places, and other things from the story).

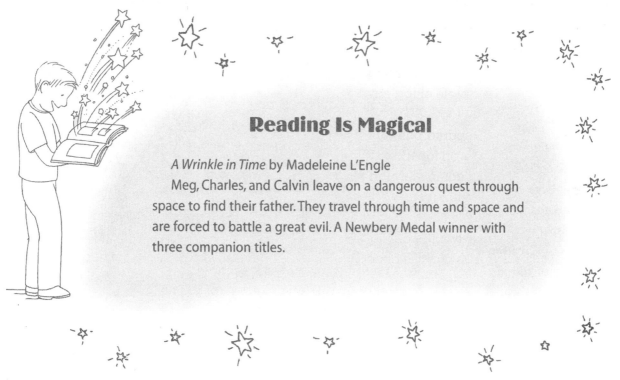

Reading Is Magical

A Wrinkle in Time by Madeleine L'Engle
Meg, Charles, and Calvin leave on a dangerous quest through space to find their father. They travel through time and space and are forced to battle a great evil. A Newbery Medal winner with three companion titles.

Materials:
A Magic Theme List
Paper
Pen or pencil
Scissors
Basket

Directions:
1. Make a Magic Theme List.
2. Cut out each item on your list, fold it up, and place it in the basket.
3. Gather your friends in a circle.
4. Choose someone to begin the tale by handing them the basket. Have that person reach into the basket and begin the story, using what's written on the slip.
5. After a minute or two, have the story-teller pass the basket to the person sitting on his or her right. That person now draws a slip of paper from the basket and continues the story, using whatever's written.
6. Continue until all the slips of paper have been drawn.
7. Instead of wrapping up the tale, the last person gets to take the tale to an exciting cliffhanger, using any story element of his or her choosing. So the tale never really ends!

Magic Plants

Carrots—Vision
Catnip—Playfulness
Cucumber—Growth
Daisies—Friendship
Lavender—Love
Marigold—Dreams
Mint—Prosperity
Nasturtiums—Creativity
Onions—Strength
Peppers—Excitement
Primroses—Resourcefulness
Rosemary—Protection
Roses—Psychic Powers
Sage—Wisdom
Strawberries—Romance
Sweet Williams—Kindness
Thyme—Healing
Tomato—Love

Spring Equinox: March 20–22

The Spring Equinox is one of the two times each year when the amount of day and night are the same everywhere. For witches and wizards, this is a time to celebrate the awakening of the earth—trees budding, chickens hatching, flowers blooming. It is the perfect time to enjoy a Mystic CinnaMint Shake, plant a Magic Garden, or play a game of Magic Slap-Clap-Snap.

Mystic CinnaMint Shake

This refreshing springtime brew will awaken your senses, and conjure up love (vanilla), joy (chocolate), prosperity (mint), and friendship (cinnamon). You'll need to double the recipe if you have a friend over.

Ingredients:
3 chocolate mint cookies
3 scoops vanilla ice cream
1 cup ice-cold milk
1 cinnamon stick

Directions:
1. Break up the cookies.
2. In a tall glass, layer the cookies and ice cream.
3. Add the milk, and use the cinnamon stick to mix.

Planting a Magic Garden

If you didn't plant a Magic Garden earlier in the book, then now would be a good time to try it. This Magic Garden is done in pots. Be sure to choose ones with a hole in the bottom for good drainage.

Materials:

3 planting pots	Paint
Paintbrush	Small stones
Potting soil	Crumbled eggshells
3, 6, or 9 plants	Water
Plant food	

Directions:

1. Paint something magical on the pots. For example, magic symbols, magic animals, or even a magic spell you have made up.

    Let the paint dry thoroughly before planting.

2. Add a few small stones (or pieces of broken pots) in the bottom, before adding the potting mix. This will help with the drainage.

3. Put a scoop of potting soil in each pot. Mix in the crumbled eggshells.

4. Place 1 to 3 plants in each pot, depending on the size of the pot.

5. Fill with potting soil, add a little plant food, and water thoroughly. Place a dish (slightly larger than the bottom of the pot) under the pot, to help the plant retain water. This is particularly important if you live in a dry, hot climate.

6. Make up a spell to help your new plants grow.
    Or try saying these words over the plants:
    Earth and water and Sun so bright,
    Help these plants grow overnight!   (continued)

FUN FACT

Plants Get Thirsty!

Water your plants when the topsoil feels dry to the touch. Try to water in the morning or early evening, rather than during the hottest time of the day. If the leaves begin to yellow, the plant is probably getting too much water, or is unable to drain properly. If the leaves begin to droop, the plant needs more water, or is not absorbing the water. If this happens, try placing the pot in a pan of water, letting the plant soak the water up through its roots.

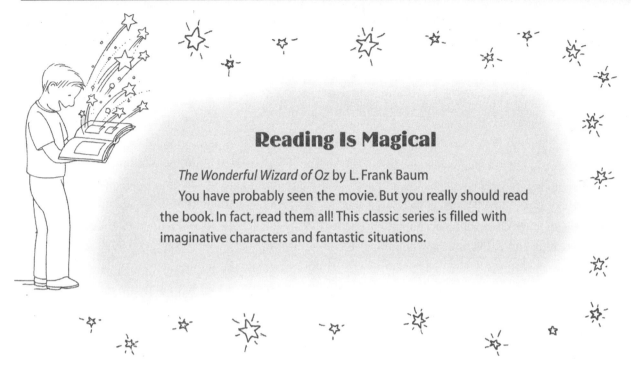

Reading Is Magical

The Wonderful Wizard of Oz by L. Frank Baum
You have probably seen the movie. But you really should read the book. In fact, read them all! This classic series is filled with imaginative characters and fantastic situations.

Magic Garden pots make excellent gifts. You can give two of them away, and still have one left for yourself!

Magic Slap-Clap-Snap

This is a fun, lively game, requiring a quick, observant mind, and a good memory. You can choose any theme for this game, but during the Spring Equinox, it is always fun to play using the "First Signs of Spring."

Here's how to play:
1. Gather a group of friends in a circle.
2. On the count of three, have everyone in the circle slap both their hands on the tops of their legs, clap their hands together, then snap their fingers. Start with a slow pace.
3. Choose someone to start. The next time everyone's fingers snap, that person tells, in a word or two, what he or she thinks is a first sign of Spring. For example, "Baby chicks!"
4. The next time fingers snap, the person to the right must come up with an idea. If he or she can't, or repeats something that's already been used, that person has to drop out of the circle.
5. As the game continues, pick up the pace of the slap, clap, snap, so that everyone has to think faster.
6. The last person who can think of a new sign of Spring (in a snap!) wins!

Chapter 12

A Calendar of Magic:
Maypole Festival to the Fall Equinox

Maypole Festival: May 1

A colorful Maypole is usually the center of this celebration. Considered the second most important event of the magical year, the Maypole Festival celebrates all living things— plants (which are now in full bloom), animals (whose babies are now starting to make their own way in the world), and those we love (who make our lives richer and fuller). The colors of the Maypole remind witches and wizards that it's also a time to celebrate diversity. This is a great time of year to do something special for your mother, and any other girls or women who make your life magical. You might want to make them Maypole Truffles or a Maypole Wishing Hoop. You might even invite them to a Magical Maypole Tea.

Maypole Truffles

Originally, chocolate truffles were home-made, bite-size treats, *without* a hard chocolate shell. In that tradition, these white chocolate truffles are easy to make, and will bring a rainbow of happiness to all who make or eat them! This recipe makes about 20 truffles.

Ingredients:
8 ounces white chocolate, chopped into
  small pieces
3 tablespoons heavy cream
2 tablespoons fruit preserves
½ cup rainbow sprinkles or candy confetti

Directions:
1. Place the white chocolate in a mixing bowl.
2. Heat the cream in a saucepan, just until it begins to simmer.
3. Pour the cream over the chocolate, let stand for 1 minute, and then stir until smooth. Be *extra* careful not to get any water or steam in the chocolate. If you do, the chocolate will harden, and there's no remedy; you just have to start over.
4. Continue stirring while adding your favorite flavor of seedless fruit preserves.
5. Place in an airtight plastic container and refrigerate overnight.
6. Line a cookie sheet with wax paper. Pour the sprinkles or candy confetti into a wide bowl.
7. With cool, dry hands, scoop a teaspoon of the chocolate out, roll it into a ball quickly, and cover it with rainbow sprinkles or candy confetti.
8. Refrigerate until ready to devour!

What a sweet magical surprise for your mother or other special someone!

Maypole Wishing Hoop

This magical helper is even more fun than dancing around a Maypole! And you can use this hoop year-round by hanging it over your bed, your desk, or a favorite reading chair. It is sure to brighten any room.

Materials:
12-inch hoop
Scissors
6 lengths of ribbon (1 inch by 12 feet)
12 lengths of ribbon (½ inch by 12 feet)

Directions:
1. Choose a hoop. It can be made of wood, metal, or plastic. Just make sure it's lightweight and sturdy. Choose ribbons in a rainbow of colors.
2. Loop a ribbon around the hoop, so the length of ribbon is divided in half. *Make a wish,* as you tie a knot, securing the ribbon to the hoop. Clip each of the two ribbon ends at an angle and knot (so that they don't unravel), *repeating your wish* with each knot.

Magical Tip

Increase the Wishing Hoop's magical power by coordinating the color of the ribbon with the intent of your wish.

3. Tie the next length of ribbon next to the previous length, *making another wish!* Continue, alternating the color or width of ribbon, until the hoop is completely covered.
4. Say these words over your wishing hoop:
   Wishing Hoop of every hue,
   Help make all my wishes come true!

A wishing hoop would make a most thoughtful gift.

A Magical Maypole Tea

This festival party is a way to do something special for the girls and women who make your life magical, as well as a way to bring more magic into everyone's lives.

To make Magical Teas, add one or more of the following ingredients to any basic tea:

Orange—Joy	Mint—Prosperity
Lemon—Creativity	Strawberry—Romance
Apple—Health	Almond—Wisdom
Allspice—Playfulness	Cinnamon—Friendship

Materials:
Construction paper
Colorful pens or pencils
Magical Teas
Cookies or mini-sandwiches or treats

(continued)

Directions:

1. Gather a group of friends and decide on a date, a place, and an invitation list that includes girls and women who make your lives special.
2. Using the construction paper and colorful pens or pencils, make invitations. In the invitation ask that the recipient bring the materials needed to make a Maypole Wishing Hoop.
3. On the day of the event, decorate the party site in a rainbow of colors. Hang a Maypole Wishing Hoop in the center of the room, lifting and attaching each ribbon strand to a wall or the ceiling, so that it forms a colorful canopy.
4. Have each party-planning friend bring cookies, mini-sandwiches, or treats— and teapots to brew a variety of Magical Teas.
5. When your guests arrive, seat them next to the friend who invited them. When everyone has arrived, have each friend introduce themselves and the special guest(s) they invited.
6. Serve the teas and goodies, and let everyone chat.
7. When everyone has had a cup of tea, clear a space in front of each guest to make a Maypole Wishing Hoop. You can either have one person show the group each simple step, or each party-planning friend can show the guest(s) he or she invited.

Magical Tip

It would be fun and helpful to have little cards at each guest's place that tell them about the Magical Teas, and another that tells them how to match ribbon colors with the intent of their wishes.

9. When all the Maypole Wishing Hoops are completed, have everyone at the party hold up their Wishing Hoop, and say (all together):
   Wishing hoop of every hue,
   Help make all our wishes come true!

Summer Solstice: June 20–22

The Summer Solstice is often called the longest day of the year. This is a celebration of the fruits of nature, and of the magic that animals bring to our lives. Pets and Familiars are welcomed at this festival, and magic herbs are harvested. It is also a time of giving away things we've grown, whether it's something from nature (herbs, flowers, fruit), something we've made (pictures, crafts, or projects), or something we feel (telling someone we like or love them). This is also the time to do something special for your father, and any other boys or men who make your life magical. You might make them Peanut Butter Hedgehog Truffles or a Magic Power Pouch. You could even ask them to join you on a Magical Rescue.

Peanut Butter Hedgehog Truffles

Here's another easy recipe for irresistible truffles. These milk-chocolate bites will melt the hearts of the magical boys or men in your life. This recipe makes about 20 truffles.

Ingredients:
8 ounces milk chocolate, chopped into
    small pieces
¼ cup heavy cream
2 tablespoons peanut butter, creamy or
    crunchy
1 cup mini semisweet chocolate chips

Directions:
1. Place the chocolate in a mixing bowl.
2. Heat the cream in a saucepan, just until it begins to simmer.
3. Pour the cream over the chocolate, let stand for 1 minute, and then stir until smooth. Be *extra* careful not to get any water or steam in the chocolate. If you do, the chocolate will harden, and there's no remedy; you just have to start over.
4. Continue stirring while adding peanut butter.
5. Place the mixture in an airtight plastic container and refrigerate overnight.
6. Line a cookie sheet with wax paper. Pour the mini chocolate chips into a wide bowl.
7. With cool, dry hands, scoop a teaspoon of the chocolate out, roll it into a ball quickly, and cover with mini "hedgehog" chips!
8. Refrigerate until ready to devour!

These are too good to last very long at your house.

Magic Power Pouch

Everyone can use a Magic Power Pouch, especially the boys and men in your life who lend a heart or a hand, whenever you need it. This might be the perfect gift for one of them.

Materials:
¼ yard sturdy fabric
Pen or chalk
Scissors
Needle and thread
Fabric glue
Pins
12-inch length of cord
3 power beads
Fabric paint or decorations

(continued)

Directions:

1. Choose a fabric that will be durable, like corduroy or heavy cotton. You can choose something in a solid color and decorate it, or choose a fabric that already has magical pictures or a magical print on it.

2. Fold the fabric in half, so the right sides are facing each other. Draw a "U" (with pen or chalk) that is approximately 5 inches wide by 7 inches deep. Pin the fabric together on the inside of the "U" (to hold the two pieces in place). Cut the "U" out.

3. Thread your needle and stitch a straight line around the "U," approximately ½ inch from the edge, leaving a 2-inch opening at the top of one side. Take all the pins out.

4. Glue the sides of the opening down against each side of the pouch.

5. Fold the top of the "U" down approximately 1 inch. Glue the bottom edge down, leaving a pocket or opening above for the cord.

6. When the glue is dry, turn the pouch right side out, and thread the cord through the hidden opening along the top edge.

7. Thread the two ends of the cord through one power bead (pony beads, available at craft stores, work well). This will allow the user to slide and hold the pouch closed.

8. At each end of the cord, tie a knot approximately 2 inches from the bottom. Add a power bead and tie another knot to secure the bead in place and to keep the cord from unraveling.

9. Decorate the power pouch

Give the pouch to someone really special. They are sure to wonder at all the work you put into making it!

Magic Rescues

One of the things the Summer Solstice celebrates is pets and the magic they bring into our lives. However, many pets don't have loving homes. For these pets, agencies have been set up to help. You probably already know about the SPCA (or "the Pound"). There are also private, nonprofit rescue agencies for almost every breed of dog or cat. You can find out about these agencies through friends, breeders, vets, or the Internet. Together with an adult, you could make a difference for these animals.

Here's what to do.

1. Contact a rescue agency and ask how you can help. They may need help posting signs, stuffing envelopes, or finding homes or foster homes for pets.

2. Ask your dad, grandpa, or another boy or man who brings magic into your life to help with you for an hour or two.

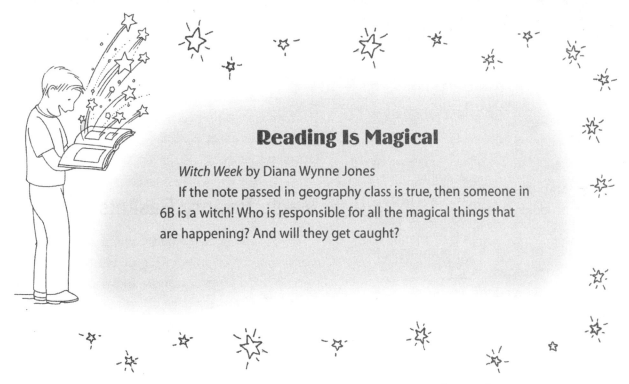

Reading Is Magical

Witch Week by Diana Wynne Jones
If the note passed in geography class is true, then someone in 6B is a witch! Who is responsible for all the magical things that are happening? And will they get caught?

3. Volunteer with a smile. Do whatever the agency asks you to do—and do it to the best of your abilities.
4. Ask a person at the agency to take a picture of you with the friend who volunteered with you, the new friends you made through the agency, or the pet or pets you helped!
5. Put your pictures into your Magic Book as a reminder of your good deed.

Magic Thanksgiving: August 1

During this Festival, witches and wizards give thanks for all the good things in their lives. This festival marks the beginning of the harvest season.. It is a great time to appreciate the family and friends you have, and maybe do something for someone else a little less fortunate. You could bake some Magic Harvest Cookies, make some Magic Bounty Baskets, or lead family and friends in a Circle of Thanks.

Magic Harvest Cookies

These crunchy, chewy treats contain the bounty from harvests around the world! This recipe makes about 60 cookies.

Ingredients:
1 ½ cups flour
1 teaspoon baking powder
1 teaspoon baking soda
¼ teaspoon salt
1 cup butter or vegetable shortening
1 ½ cups dark brown sugar
1 cup granulated sugar
2 eggs
1 teaspoon vanilla
½ cup bran
1 ½ cups rolled oats
¾ cup chopped mixed nuts
¾ cup dried fruit bits, raisins, or glazed
    fruit bits
¾ cup shredded coconut

Directions:
1. Preheat your oven to 375 degrees. Use nonstick cookie sheets.
2. Sift together the flour, baking powder, baking soda, and salt. Set aside.
3. Cream together the butter and sugars.
4. Beat in the eggs and vanilla.
5. Fold in the flour mixture, ¼ cup at a time, the bran, and the oats.
6. Fold in the nuts, fruit bits, and coconut.

7. Scoop a teaspoonful of thick batter onto the cookie sheet. Flatten slightly. Bake for approximately 15 minutes, until golden brown. Cool on wire racks.

Pass these out to all the people you are thankful to know.

Magic Bounty Baskets

This is a magical way to celebrate all the wonderful things in your life by sharing with people a little less fortunate than you. Magic Bounty Baskets are sure to bring a smile to the face of whoever receives them.

Materials:
Plastic strawberry basket
3 lengths of ribbon (¼ inch by 18 inches)
Green crinkle shred
Magic Bounty:
    Small pieces of washed fresh fruit
            (grapes, cherries, strawberries)
    Bite-size cookies, dried fruit, or nuts
    Small toys, crayons, drawing pads,
            puzzles, bubbles
    Small stuffed animals
    Small musical instruments
    A small pot of flowers

Directions:
1. Make sure your basket is clean.
2. Starting at the center front and top of the basket, thread a ribbon in and out,

in a straight line that parallels the top of the basket. When you reach the center front again, pull the two ends of the ribbon so they are even and tie a bow, *making a wish*, for the future owner. Do this again with each of the remaining two strands of ribbon, leaving a small space between the ribbons.

3. Build a thin nest within your Magical Bounty Basket with the green (for luck) crinkle shred.
4. Add your Magic Bounty!
5. Say these words over your basket:
   Bring good fortune to those in need,
   So, someday, they may thrive and lead.

Donate your baskets to a local children's hospital or homeless shelter. Remember to call ahead to be sure they will accept them.

Circle of Thanks

Sometimes, we don't recognize, or we lose track of, some of the simple things in life for which we should be grateful. And sometimes we can see what our friends should be thankful for more easily than we see what we should be thankful for in our own lives. To form a Circle of Thanks, gather some friends or your family, and of course some harvest treats and drinks. Then follow these directions:

1. Gather around a table filled with harvest treats.

2. Choose someone to begin. That person will talk about something he or she admires about the person sitting to his or her right, something for which that person should be thankful. The "something" can be a talent or personality trait (like creativity, wisdom, or a great sense of humor). Or it can be something like twinkling blue eyes, a beautiful smile, a comfortable home, or special friends.
3. Then the person who was just talked about gets a minute to talk about the person to his or her right, until you work your way around the table!
4. When everyone has gotten a chance to speak, it's time to enjoy the harvest treats!

Fall Equinox: September 20–22

This is the second time of the year when day and night are the same length everywhere. This festival celebrates the full Fall harvest, when all fields are cleared and prepared for the approaching winter. This is a time to clear unwanted or unneeded things out of your life, replacing them with things that will enrich your life through the cold days ahead. You may decide to treat yourself to a Magic Misfit

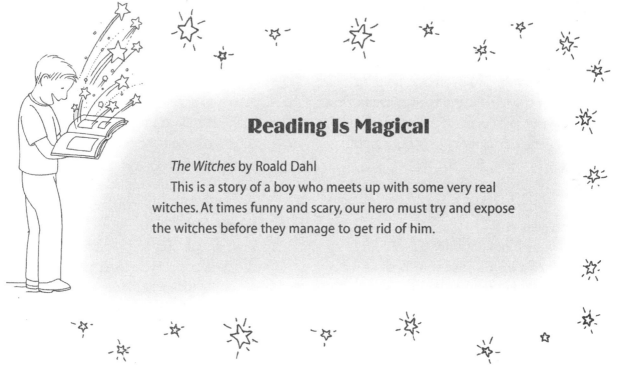

Reading Is Magical

The Witches by Roald Dahl
This is a story of a boy who meets up with some very real witches. At times funny and scary, our hero must try and expose the witches before they manage to get rid of him.

Pizza. You may create some Magic Misfit Stories and throw a Magic Misfit Auction.

Magic Misfit Pizza

Here's a dessert pizza that will help you get rid of all those pesky treats that are cluttering up your cupboard!

Crust ingredients:
1¼ cups flour
½ teaspoon baking soda
½ teaspoon salt
½ cup butter

½ cup light brown sugar
⅓ cup granulated sugar
1 egg
½ teaspoon vanilla

Filling ingredients:
8 ounces cream cheese
2 tablespoons butter
½ cup powdered sugar
¼ cup heavy cream

Misfit toppings: M&M's, chocolate chips, mini marshmallows, fruit, nuts, coconut, crumbled cookies, crumbled candy bars

Directions:

1. Preheat your oven to 350 degrees. Lightly butter a 12-inch round pizza pan, and dust with flour.
2. Sift together flour, baking soda, and salt. Set aside.
3. Cream together butter (½ cup) and the sugars.
4. Beat in the egg and vanilla.
5. Fold in the flour mixture, ¼ cup at a time.
6. Spread the mixture in the pizza pan and bake for 20 to 25 minutes, or until golden brown. Set on wire racks to cool.
7. With a mixer on a high setting, whip the cream cheese, 2 tablespoons of butter, and powdered sugar until fluffy.
8. Turn the mixer to a low setting, and mix in the heavy cream, just until blended.
9. Spread the mixture on the cooling pizza and top with all your magical misfit treats!

You may just decide you have to have this treat more than once a year!

Magic Misfit Stories

One of the fun ways to clear out unneeded things, while raising money for a special project or charity, is to have a Magic Misfit Auction. A Magic Misfit Auction is like a white elephant sale, only it is more creative and more fun!

The first thing you need to do is collect the Magic Misfits. These can be books, toys, furniture, knick-knacks—anything that people are willing to give away. After you have a whole bunch of them, you will need to do a very important thing for each one—make up a story for it. You can make up these stories yourself, or get all of your friends to come up with ideas.

Materials:
Magic Misfits you've collected
Your imagination
Colorful paper
Pens or pencils
6-inch lengths of ribbon
Hole punch

Directions:

1. Focus on one Magic Misfit at a time. Make up a story that will convince someone to bid for that Misfit and take it home. The wilder, funnier, or more heartwarming the story, the better. If you're stuck for ideas, start by looking for inspiration from some of your favorite stories. For example, say you have to make up a story for an old battered frying pan, think about Beauty and the Beast!

My name is Armand Penne.

I was once the most famous chef in all of France. But then an Evil Sorcerer, jealous of my talent, turned me into this wretched pan. I cannot return to my former self until I help a Beast turn into a Prince, by preparing a delicious, magical meal for someone special!

2. Write down the story and use the ribbon to attach the story to the Magic Misfit!

Magic Misfits Auction

Does your soccer team need new equipment? Does your school or class need a fundraiser? How would you like to raise some money for your favorite charity? Here's a way to raise money, clear out clutter, and have fun.

What you'll need:
A group of friends
A place to hold the auction
Poster board or paper
Pens or paint and brushes
Tape or push pins
Donation receipts
Raffle entry box
Cash box
Plates, cups, napkins
Refreshments

What to do:
1. Decide on a date and a location. (Be sure to get permission to use the location.)
2. Make and put up posters advertising the event. If you want to sell tickets to the Auction, number and design the tickets (with room for a name, address, and phone number), so you can hold a raffle at the end of the bidding. And decorate a box to hold the raffle entries.
3. Collect unwanted or unneeded items from your own room, family, friends, teachers, or neighbors. (Remember to give receipts if the money raised will go to a nonprofit cause.)
4. Write Magic Misfit Stories for each item.
5. Select an auctioneer. Plan time for the event-planners to take turns introducing and telling the stories of the Magic Misfits—and plan the order in which the Misfits will be auctioned.
6. You may want to keep a few items aside for raffle prizes in case everything is sold.
7. Make or have bite-size refreshments donated. You want your guests to be able to eat with their fingers without getting messy. And be sure to have enough plates, cups, and napkins on hand. Happy, well-fed attendees are more generous bidders!

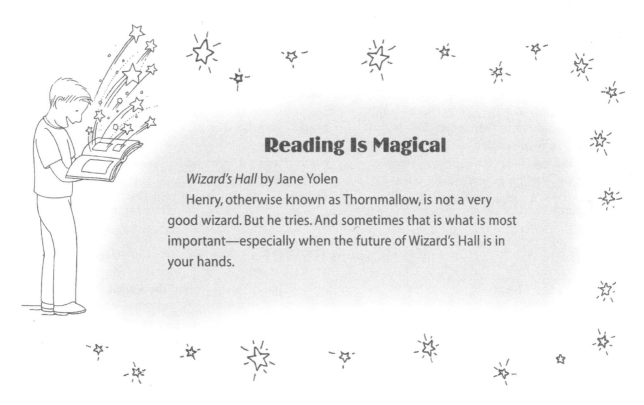

Reading Is Magical

Wizard's Hall by Jane Yolen
Henry, otherwise known as Thornmallow, is not a very
good wizard. But he tries. And sometimes that is what is most
important—especially when the future of Wizard's Hall is in
your hands.

8. When everyone is gathered, thank
everyone for coming and tell them how
the money that you raise will be used.
Then, let the auction begin! Keep it fun
with a quick pace, lots of enthusiasm
when telling the stories, and lots of
laughs and pats on the back.

9. At the end of the auction, use those
items that were not sold, or those
item(s) that are donated back by the
people who bought them, as the prizes
for the raffle!

10. Remember to thank everyone again, to
invite them to start saving Magic
Misfits for next year's auction, and to
give receipts for all purchases and
donations!

11. Secure the money you made, put the
location back the way you found it, and
celebrate your accomplishment!

Glossary

astrology—the study of the influence that the stars and planets are supposed to have on people and events.

cast—to send or put forth, as in a spell.

cauldron—a large black iron pot.

charms—objects or words that are supposed to have magical powers.

equinox—the two times of the year when the length of day and night are the same everywhere.

Familiar—a creature or pet that lives with a witch or a wizard and helps with the practice of magic.

herbs—a plant valued for its medicinal qualities.

numerology—the study of the hidden significance of numbers.

omen—a sign or indication.

palmistry—the art of reading a person's character or future from the markings on his palms.

potion—a liquid mixture.

prism—cut glass that disperses light into its separate colors.

solstice—the two times of the year when the sun is closest or farthest away from the earth.

spell—a word or words supposed to have magic powers.

witch or **wizard**—terms used to describe people with magical abilities.

zodiac—an imaginary belt in the heavens.

Puzzle Answers

page 3 • Three's the Charm

page 4 • Magical Word Search

page 11 • A Robe Filled with Magic

Puzzle Answers

page 15 • **Which Wand Is Which?**

page 36 • **Twisted Magic**

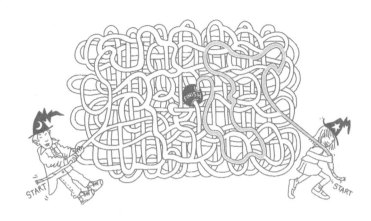

page 23 • **Today Is Your Lucky Day**

page 40 • **Mis-spelling Spell**

page 44 • **Magic Friendship Bundles**

1. D	2. C
3. F	4. B
5. A	6. E
7. G	

page 45 • **Mmm–Mmm Magic**

page 25 • **If You Wish**

Puzzle Answers

page 52 • Picture This

"I want to be a better reader"

page 59 • Mini Vision Bubble Maze

page 96 • You Look Familiar

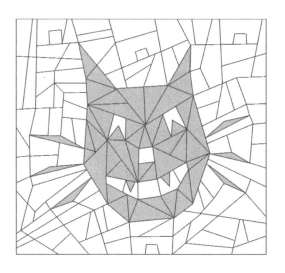

page 109 • Magic Hink Pinks

FLUID DRUID
BLIZZARD WIZARD
STITCH WITCH

page 85 • Brain Power

	O	A	R		I										
M	M	K	R		M	R		B			O	H			
P	B	O	O	S	E	C	M	L	Y	A	T	D	E		
S	R	U	E	T	T	E	T	B	R	E	I	N	I	R	S
H	A	A	C	T	L	Y	A	Y	R	P	A	W	E	N	G
M	A	K	E		M	Y		B	R	A	I	N			
S	M	A	R	T	E	R		B	Y		T	H	E		
H	O	U	R		−	L	E	T		R	E	A	D	I	N	G
	B	O	O	S	T		M	Y							
P	R	A	C	T	I	C	A	L			P	O	W	E	R	S

Wishing on a Star Template

Trace this star on construction paper, and then decorate it to create your own wishing star (spell on page 71).

We Have EVERYTHING!®

Available wherever books are sold!

Everything® **After College Book**
$12.95, 1-55850-847-3

Everything® **Astrology Book**
$12.95, 1-58062-062-0

Everything® **Baby Names Book**
$12.95, 1-55850-655-1

Everything® **Baby Shower Book**
$12.95, 1-58062-305-0

Everything® **Barbeque Cookbook**
$12.95, 1-58062-316-6

Everything® **Bartender's Book**
$9.95, 1-55850-536-9

Everything® **Bedtime Story Book**
$12.95, 1-58062-147-3

Everything® **Beer Book**
$12.95, 1-55850-843-0

Everything® **Bicycle Book**
$12.95, 1-55850-706-X

Everything® **Build Your Own Home Page**
$12.95, 1-58062-339-5

Everything® **Casino Gambling Book**
$12.95, 1-55850-762-0

Everything® **Cat Book**
$12.95, 1-55850-710-8

Everything® **Christmas Book**
$15.00, 1-55850-697-7

Everything® **College Survival Book**
$12.95, 1-55850-720-5

Everything® **Cover Letter Book**
$12.95, 1-58062-312-3

Everything® **Crossword and Puzzle Book**
$12.95, 1-55850-764-7

Everything® **Dating Book**
$12.95, 1-58062-185-6

Everything® **Dessert Book**
$12.95, 1-55850-717-5

Everything® **Dog Book**
$12.95, 1-58062-144-9

Everything® **Dreams Book**
$12.95, 1-55850-806-6

Everything® **Etiquette Book**
$12.95, 1-55850-807-4

Everything® **Family Tree Book**
$12.95, 1-55850-763-9

Everything® **Fly-Fishing Book**
$12.95, 1-58062-148-1

Everything® **Games Book**
$12.95, 1-55850-643-8

Everything® **Get-a-Job Book**
$12.95, 1-58062-223-2

The ultimate reference for couples planning their wedding!

- Scheduling, budgeting, etiquette, hiring caterers, florists, and photographers
- Ceremony & reception ideas
- Over 100 forms and checklists
- And much, much more!

$12.95, 384 pages, 8" x 9 ¼"

Personal finance made easy—and fun!

- Create a budget you can live with
- Manage your credit cards
- Set up investment plans
- Money-saving tax strategies
- And much, much more!

$12.95, 288 pages, 8" x 9 ¼"

For more information, or to order, call 800-872-5627
or visit www.adamsmedia.com/everything

Adams Media Corporation, 260 Center Street, Holbrook, MA 02343

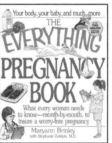

**For more information, or to order, call 800-872-5627
or visit www.adamsmedia.com/everything**

Adams Media Corporation, 260 Center Street, Holbrook, MA 02343